Is Music

BOOKS BY JOHN TAGGART

POETRY

Is Music: Selected Poems
There Are Birds
Crosses: Poems 1992–1998
Pastorelles
When the Saints
Standing Wave
Prompted
Loop
Dehiscence
Peace on Earth
Dodeka
Prism and the Pine Twig
The Pyramid Is a Pure Crystal
To Construct a Clock

PROSE

*Songs of Degrees: Essays on Contemporary Poetry
      and Poetics*
*Remaining in Light: Ant Meditations on a Painting
      by Edward Hopper*

TRANSLATION

Aeschylus/Fragments

Is Music

SELECTED POEMS

John Taggart

Edited by Peter O'Leary
Foreword by C.D. Wright

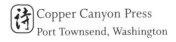 Copper Canyon Press
Port Townsend, Washington

Cover art: Jennifer Taggart, *Cucumber vine tendril,* 2009.

Selections from *Pastorelles* and *There Are Birds* are reprinted under the license from Flood Editions.

Part 1 of "Kitaj Angels" was first published in *Colorado Review,* part 2 in *Hambone.* The entire sequence first appeared in the online magazine *LRL* (http://www .littleredleaves.com).

The author wishes to thank Alyssa Martinez and Minami Furukawa for their assistance in preparing the manuscript.

Some of my poems—because they are book-length and entire books in themselves—cannot be included in this collection. To present a part or parts of them is to misrepresent them.—JT

Copper Canyon Press is in residence at Fort Worden State Park in Port Townsend, Washington, under the auspices of Centrum. Centrum is a gathering place for artists and creative thinkers from around the world, students of all ages and backgrounds, and audiences seeking extraordinary cultural enrichment.

LIBRARY OF CONGRESS CATALOGING-IN-PUBLICATION DATA

Taggart, John, 1942–

Is music: selected poems / John Taggart; edited by Peter O'Leary; foreword, C.D. Wright.

    p. cm.

ISBN 978-1-55659-304-8 (pbk.: alk. paper)

I. O'Leary, Peter, 1968–   II. Title.

PS3570.A32I8 2010

811'.54 — dc22   2010004655

9 8 7 6 5 4 3 2   FIRST PRINTING

COPPER CANYON PRESS

Post Office Box 271

Port Townsend, Washington 98368 • www.coppercanyonpress.org

this book is for Jennifer, for Sarah and Holly

Contents

Listening to John

My first slow-dance with John Taggart's poetry was *Conjunctions 10*: "Marvin Gaye Suite."

I didn't know who John Taggart was, but I was cutting my R&B teeth in Memphis, Tennessee, when Marvin Gaye was The Man.

What's going on. What's going on, people.

John Taggart was born not in Guthrie Center but in Perry, Iowa.

Raised in small towns in Indiana. Son of a preacher man. Straight-up Protestant. Nothing serpent-kissy or glossolalicky.

When my family was moving to Iowa City for a year, Taggart called up those punishing Midwestern winters:

"They had to tie a rope from the house to the barn, so they could make their way to the barn and back."

"They had to beat the cows with boards to keep them from freezing to death."

(It could have been horses. Equally horrifying.)

He started the influential *Maps* when he was an undergraduate.

Went to Earlham College with the good Quakers. His senior thesis was on Wallace Stevens.

He wasn't sure what Mr. Stevens was talking about, but it sounded like some cool beans. It wasn't long before young Taggart hit upon Mr. Bronk.

What's going on here.

A fellowship to the writers' workshop in Aspen. A kid meeting writers: Toby Olson, Paul Blackburn, Bobby Byrd. His initiation had begun.

Early on, unlike some not-so-early-to-rise he knew he wanted to be a writer.

He had in mind to write fiction. French fiction.

Even new French fiction required getting people in and out of cars and clothes, opening doors, rounding corners—some sign of a narrator. So lifelike.

"The furniture moving aspects" of writing did not really appeal to him.

He wanted to get down on his knees with the language and dig with both hands.

An M.A. from the University of Chicago. A Ph.D. from Syracuse. He wrote his dissertation on Zukofsky.

Admits to growing a little tired of Zukofsky (dissertations are famous for letting the air out). Z's coldness esp. And growing more interested in Oppen. Just as exacting, but warmer.

The Taggart house in the Cumberland Valley. We visited once. It is the temperature of the place preserved in memory, the serrated air. The rushing cold millrace across the road from their house. The black cherry trees.

The scoured dark inside the covered bridge. The covered bridge of Cumberland County. Its marvelous structure.

"The truss principle + arch… the structure is / what matters the flower the music of it." (See "Pastorelle 14.")

His collection of meticulously kept tools. "The careful workman." (See "Eroded Rock, 1942.")

He gave our son, who was around seven then, a fine, old bone-handled knife.

I gave my son, who is grown now, my father's fine, old bone-handled knife.

His love of the grid. Until it all but disappears in its penciled traces. (He cites Agnes Martin.)

A fondness for musical forms, of the searching variety: *ricercar*. (See eponymously titled poem.)

Partial to simple nouns. One syllable, "child the most basic word most haunting word" (see "In True Night"); two syllables, "crystal is a basic word crystal not paradise" (ibid.). Not more than two, unless there is a *necessary* polysyllable no one could have seen coming: *pantherine*. (See "The Lily Alone.")

How did we get along without it. What's going on here, Marvin.

Easy to assemble his *company keepers* (so the lifer I met at Angola called his roses).

Taggart's roses: writers, musicians, painters, and other artists. William Bronk, George Oppen, Susan Howe, Michael Palmer, Louis Zukofsky, Robert Creeley; Elvin Jones, John Coltrane, Thelonious Monk, Sonny Rollins; Marvin Gaye, Al Green, Betty Carter, Sister Rosetta Tharpe, Clara Ward; Mark Rothko, Edward Weston, R.B. Kitaj (a shortened list). Also actual rugosas, of the should-not/must-pick varieties.

Those egghead Objectivists. Those Black Mountain cats. Those big-bosomed blues singers.

Just three words from Thomas Bernhard could set him off. A line from Thomas Traherne. Well, yeah.

Then a name that doesn't quite fit the grid, Robert Quine, ur-punk guitarist who played strong and strange for a lot of people who sucked up the glory: Richard Hell, Lou Reed, and so on.

A little poking around turns up Quine the same age as Taggart, attending Earlham, same as Taggart. I doubt if young Taggart missed much, certainly not an offensive noise escaping a dorm window.

Susceptible to the homage, the elegy, the ekphrastic. None of the terms satisfy the overall condition of this writing, esp. *ekphrastic*, which is fitting and lacking in an irritating way.

An inveterate correspondent. He continues to write his letters by hand, the script running perpendicular to the lines on the paper. It is a kind of scoring. And a kind of drawing.

Equally compositions and drawings.

A poet in the habit of writers whose letters are a highly reflective art in and of themselves.

The words are always moving, choosing phrases, singing. "To sing is to be untied." (See "Rhythm and Blues Singer.")

I am sure one knife is lost by now. More than likely, both.

The Objectivists could make things stop, stand out, and give no quarter. You would have to beat them with boards to get them to lift a limb.

Taggart likes motion: "Time for some passion in this language it's time to move / it's time to move to make a move ma—mah—moo-euve-veh." (See "The Rothko Chapel Poem.")

His signature repetition (see "Slow Song for Mark Rothko," "Giant Steps," "Peace on Earth," "Marvin Gaye Suite," and so on). "Augustine on repetition: a mode of assuring the seeker that he is on his way, and is not merely wandering blindly through the chaos from which all form arises." (See "Were You.")

Affinity for the infinitive: to breathe, to sing, to light, to give, to hold out, to stretch, to straighten, to rise, to hold out to, to take, to take into the light, to be in light, to take as the host takes, to join, to end the silence and solitude, to take into intimacy… (See "Slow Song for Mark Rothko.")

The closely monitored palette. "Forget violet." (See "Were You.") He chooses dark true colors. Ever-deepening. He likes to build them up on his blade.

Breath. That's a big topic, Marvin.

"Were you ready to listen and to understand in the gaps." (See "Were You.")

Listening to the scratch of his pen, the ping of his carriage, the bass of the speakers being balanced, the roar of his chain saw in the snag tree, and rock being laid upon rock. "The careful workman."

I was swept right up in the poem's sampling of Marvin Gaye hits, his spiraling decline, his terrible end by his father's hand. The voice carrying on and on, multitracking, lustrous and fine, feminine but with pheromones coming right out of the armpit, making the witness (like poor mad Tom watching his king go mad), making every wandering witness ("moving with the wrong rhythm on the wrong beat") want to cry. I was hooked.

— C.D. Wright

Is Music

Origin, Third Series

1969

The Drum Thing

When you listen to hear
they say
what did you see?

I saw
Egypt smothered.

She died, that entire place
stiffly in the old manner.

Drums.

In the morning stumbles her ghost
the skin off the muscles
and in moving has the skull and horns of a deer.

From the suburbs
out of an old Ford
others come with her, animal shapes in walking.

A fly-covered horse hangs from
a tree in the sun, heaved
there from a swing chain, its belly ripped out, wind now.

The grey tongue of the horse has only flies.

Lester Young Pursued by Meteors & Other Personages of the Night

for Abraham Veinus

1

Whatever
is
entirely deprived
of light—
the palm
of the hand—
goes
between when
and conditions
of almost, a-
round this great fire
presst against
the air, this
contrived
silence, night scene.

       Here are
    all the meteors
    and the faces as
    meteors
    wave
    as in deep
    water as
    giant flowers—
    say
    "Wonder's

only the attitude
of a man
passing
from one
stage to another"
(& fast)—they're
interested
in him, la
capigliatura
disfatta nella
fuga delle
costellazioni, a
messed-up
dragon-fly.

2

Of the night scene. The

figures which
fingers
of the hand
point
are not the same
in going as
appears
dark against
the brightness
in coming

back; all
comes from, goes
to, the fire
which you

perceive,
now, is
… flowers! and
above them
the figure
by the darkness,
by night.

Figures, the green meteors and other personages; figure, the man.

Is he dead enough?

And not
in the brightness,
fire, itself
undulant pink
shell, palm; he
should be half
shadow and
with a
long and regular
curve
half in ruddy
light.

    3

Water
snake, the
crab &
lesser dog: the personages
disguise
their pursuit
as a samba. Or

bathers
staggering
in sand tor-
mented
by lizards,
gradual
fish, or hunters
shooting shapeless
arrow heads,
solidified—
vermilion!—in
flight toward
the turning of the hand backwards.

Those farther away
will be done
with great
rapidity
and the aether
rushing away
from mouth-
eyes-hair should
be dyed
more deeply black
as
the final urge
of the motive
power
requires
much
leaving out.

4

Like an interview. Bother
you like cigarette
smoke in the nose
whispering
So Fletcher
I'm gone!

Why did you leap?

They had trucks going around town for all
the dances and this excited me, so I
plunged deep
into death with the whole of America.

But are you dead enough?

What do the wifes say? I say the dead
shoot the living.

That's say trapped say
sweetness, la danza della libellula.

I'd have taken off
the other night if I had five hundred dollars.

5

And *not*
in the Alvin Hotel
Broadway & 52nd St.
on the ides of,

1959, and 49 years
old just re-
turned from
Europe. No.

Here are all flowers
and faces as flowers
waves of white
emotions, say, re-
frigerator currents
conceal
the figure
of the man
half in dark…
light… like a
scene on a stage
with its
curtain burning.

Maybe there's too many flowers, maybe there's
too much smoke to breathe? Maybe
that's a get-away.

Let it all be dark… and then July! if
he's dead enough.

Position

The parade deposits
no bodies.

I walk in praise of all metals, the
aluminum cube in the desert.

Not "for no good reason, the fact only"
but the hum
the shifting absence.

To Construct a Clock

Ricercar

for Sarah, my daughter

The tribe is foreign and
their language you
didn't
know at all. It

altered in the morning
the afternoon.

You put things together.

Sanded blocks of wood
smooth blond and white
dark
brown wood

alternated, the

white began after the blond
is down the

brown when the blond
doubles, until—

"Just as smooth as riding down
the highway"—

layers
of the
river
valley, hills appear.

A fugue appears, all things and
their ornament put in angles
that remember themselves

this wood-sorrel
its five petals in your small palm.

All things are a process
procession as the first words

as what comes mutual—a pursuit
of parts
voices
after them—

unpierced simple, together…

in the beginning
in the youngest head.

The Room

So dense. The density. A reduced world.
The room…

But better, nevertheless, the waking world,
the object-poor, the edgeless.
WILLIAM BRONK

It does not have to be
but let it be
a dream: the room

is made completely of wood
several kinds
of wood, planed

whole and nearly smooth
as the machines
used to lift and position stone

for pyramids
must have been.

There is nothing between
the angles of the wood. There
are no windows, no light or air.

Surely, it is wrong to want to be here
wrong not to choose the room's opposite
the sky

where everything is approximate
and large, the ocean
which is the same as the sky.

It is even brave to do this
to remain
in the relative

except
endlessly, endlessly

to feel the directions of grain
the faint edges
where the shapes are joined

everywhere a definiteness
everywhere density.

The dream is the shape—
pure, yet enlarging—
of sensation

a definition of sensation
that is more than that
the density of

—how would you say—
the self itself
expanded, to a world.

There are no windows.

Eroded Rock, 1942

short series on a photograph by Edward Weston

1

Things endure

even in the infinite air.

2

One is sent
—through,

continuous

whole days

the newspapers
inconclusive

magazines in bright covers

letters
from friends in Maine
other poets

—sent
to the names of things

for
a kind of displacement.

3

Exactly, "representations"
a casuality at work…

this is the unknown.

4

The condition is
that the time should not
be "occupied"

warlike,
division
for maximum yield

that expectation
what comes with the chance
to move

momentum
reduced to
a circuit, the

shrill fear of obstruction
…it
must all be denied

to the end
of the accelerating wish
plastic hope itself.

5

Not the rock itself
sandstone
in a felt light, a felt scale
which is precise only in memory

the given, something
assumed as fact
made the basis of calculation
photograph.

6

"I tried the light from the opposite side in the next morning
light,—brilliant sun through muslin. Better! And more failures,
this time sheer thoughtlessness: a background of picture back-
ing was placed too close and came into focus when stopped down
which I could not see but should have realized, the corrugations
plainly show and spoil the feeling. So I have made eight negatives
from the same angle and still must go on."

Weston, patient, insistent—
high contrast on slick paper
the rock
against its own shadows—
the photograph is clear.

An art povera
deliberate, the
final gift from any man
to admit
it is all a dissatisfaction.

It is not easy, by no means
to say this—
who does not honor the careful workman—
but insistent
to see again where we are.

7

To see again…

it is more complicated, hard
than that
to leave this photograph of sandstone
its shapes bones
magical tools, pliers
whose use now is not understood…

enlarged to the labyrinths
that appear
when cities are cut in half
—an aerial view—;
the views are endless as metaphor
and the same problem

that each sign
put against the thing
is a focus and
a necessary increase in distance.
The names get us through
the days

which is not enough and too much.
We must leave the photograph.
Its craft is

only to return us
here, to looking at grey shale
in a humid river valley.

Prism and the Pine Twig

1977

Good-bye

It's time to say good-bye.

Good-bye
to the sea urchin's dried-up test, the fossil fern's
white spine embossed on grey shale

to the railroad spike
to the mantis egg-sac stuck in an orange pot

good-bye to all my desk loves, good-bye

to the spider, real spider moving on Sarah's painting
of "nothing, a treasure map"

good-bye to Jennifer, my wife, who is beautiful
and who will not understand
my beautiful daughters who will not understand

to the walls of my room, walls
of our narrow house
in a valley made by a river and blue mountains.

There are other loves, good-bye to the others.

It's time
I become Archimedes' man, the total outsider, moon-man
going away

in a rocket
like a lighted car across Kansas at night

to the real black hole
through the last blackness where the roots are
where the words' roots are

resplendent

each a light, the words wear suits of light

each assembly of letters
reduced to splendid bones and tendons
reduced to their "ordinary life"

until the secret parent appears.

Then I will be guided
to their bright particular music, flute and bell music
which is magic.

It is Tamino's, Papageno's music.
It is the root words' music.

And less than words, the roots
themselves separate
a few notes in a few minutes, 4th of July flares:

ar is laborer, is ἀρῶ, aro, to ear;
ἔργον, ars, work
and to earn.

I am no more than the careful workman.

The roots combine, words'
music defeats the queen serpent darkness

lighting the searching son's way
back to, where my loves are.

Such is my trust.
Good-bye, good-bye.

Peace on Earth

1981

Slow Song for Mark Rothko

1

To breathe and stretch one's arms again

to breathe through the mouth to breathe to

breathe through the mouth to utter in

the most quiet way not to whisper not to whisper

to breathe through the mouth in the most quiet way to

breathe to sing to breathe to sing to breathe

to sing the most quiet way.

To sing to light the most quiet light in darkness

radiantia radiantia

singing light in darkness.

To sing as the host sings in his house.

To breathe through the mouth to breathe through the

mouth to breathe to sing to

sing in the most quiet way to

sing *the seeds in the earth breathe forth*

not to whisper *the seeds* not to whisper *in the earth*

to sing *the seeds in the earth* the most quiet way to

sing *the seeds in the earth breathe forth.*

To sing to light the most quiet light in darkness

radiant light of *seeds in the earth*

singing light in the darkness.

To sing as the host sings in his house.

To breathe through the mouth to breathe to sing

in the most quiet way not to

whisper *the seeds in the earth breathe forth*

to sing totality of *the seeds* not to eat to

sing *the seeds in the earth* to

be at ease to sing totality totality

to sing to be at ease.

To sing to light the most quiet light in darkness

be at ease with radiant *seeds*

with singing light in darkness.

To sing as the host sings in his house.

2

To breathe and stretch one's arms again

to stretch to stretch to straighten to stretch to

rise to stretch to straighten to rise

to full height not to torture not to torture to

rise to full height to give to hold out to

to give the hand to hold out the hand

to give to hold out to.

To give self-lighted flowers in the darkness

fiery saxifrage

to hold out self-lighted flowers in darkness.

To give as the host gives in his house.

To stretch to stretch to straighten to stretch to

rise to full height not to torture not to

to rise to give to hold out to

give the hand to hold out the hand to give

hope hope of hope of perfect hope of perfect rest

to give hope of perfect rest

to give to hold out to.

To give self-lighted flowers in the darkness

perfect and fiery hope

to hold out lighted flowers in darkness.

To give as the host gives in his house.

To stretch to stretch to straighten to stretch to

rise to full height not to torture to

give the hand to hold out the hand to

give hope to give hope of perfect rest to

rest not to lay flat not to lay out

to rest as *seeds* as *seeds in the earth*

to give rest to hold out to.

To give self-lighted flowers in the darkness

fiery hope of perfect rest

to hold out light flowers in darkness.

To give as the host gives in his house.

3

To breathe and stretch one's arms again

to join arm in arm to join arm in arm to

join to take to take into

to join to take into a state of intimacy

not in anger not in anger

to join arm in arm to join arms

to take into intimacy.

To take into the light in the darkness

into the excited phosphor

to be in light in the darkness.

To take as the host takes into his house.

To join arm in arm to join arm in arm to

join to take to take into

to join to take into a state of intimacy

not anger not anger

to take as *the earth* takes *seeds* as

the poor the poor must be taken into

to take into intimacy.

To take into the light in the darkness

into the phosphor star-flowers

to be in the light in the darkness.

To take as the host takes into his house.

To join arm in arm to join arm in arm to

join arms to take to take into a state of intimacy

not anger

to take as *the earth* takes *seeds* as

the poor must be taken into

to end the silence and the solitude

to take into intimacy.

To take into the light in the darkness

into star-flowers before sunrise

to be in light in the darkness.

To take as the host takes into his house.

Giant Steps

1

To want to be a saint to want to be a saint to want to

to want to be a saint to be the snake-tailed one to want to

be snake-tailed with wings to be a snake-tailed saint with wings to

want to be a saint to want to awaken men wake men from nightmare.

To go down to raise to go down to raise to go to go down the

ladder to go down as taught as dance steps taught by the master as

taught to dance to step-dance to dance with giant steps to go to dance to

step-dance to dance with giant steps as taught by the master to

dance to go down the ladder to go down to raise men from nightmare.

2

To want to be a saint to want to be a saint to want to

to be snake-tailed with wings to be a snake-tailed saint with

wings to leap upon the horse-headed woman the blue-eyed woman

who chokes the throat to want to be a saint to wake men from nightmare.

To go down to raise to go down to raise to go to go down the

ladder to go down as taught by the master as taught to dance to

step-dance to dance with giant steps to dance with giant steps

down the ladder to dance down as taught by the master to dance down the

ladder to obtain possession to go down to raise men from nightmare.

3

To want to be a saint to want to be a saint to want to

to want to be a snake-tailed saint with wings to leap upon the horse-

headed woman the blue-eyed woman the woman with the little moon

who chokes the throat to want to be a saint to wake men from nightmare.

To go down to raise to go down to raise to go to go down the

ladder to go to dance as taught by the master to dance to step-dance to

dance with giant steps to dance with giant steps to dance down the

ladder as taught by the master to obtain possession to dance down to

raise men with a horn to go down to raise men from nightmare.

4

To want to be a saint to want to be a saint to want to

be a snake-tailed saint with wings to leap upon the horse-headed the

blue-eyed woman with the little moon the woman with nine shadows

who chokes the throat to want to be a saint to wake men from nightmare.

To go down to raise to go down to raise to go to go down the

ladder to dance as taught by the master to step-dance to dance with

giant steps to dance with giant steps to dance down as taught by the

master to obtain possession to dance down to raise men with a horn a

tenor horn to go to go down to raise men from nightmare.

Peace on Earth

1

To love to love those to love those who

are in to love those who are in a condition

in a condition

of hiding to love those who are in

a condition of hiding to

love those as children as the

valiant children who have gone into hiding

children who hide in a house from the roaring.

Care touches the face, untwists the face.

To love those as children who hide to

lay down to lay down with

the children to lay down with the children

in a flame to lay down in a flame of fire.

To love to love those to love those who

are in a condition a condition of hiding

to love those who are in

hiding to love those as children

valiant children who have gone into

hiding who hide in a house from the roaring

of bones in confusion

roaring of bones marching in confusion.

Care touches the face, untwists the face.

To love those who hide from the confusion

to lay down with the children

in a flame in a flame of fire to

be in to be at home with the children.

To love to love those to love those who

are in a condition of hiding

to love those who are in

hiding to love those as valiant children

who have gone into

hiding who hide in a house from the roaring

of bones the roaring of bones marching in confusion

bones marching in napalm in napalm.

Care touches the face, untwists the face.

To love those who hide from the napalm

to lay down in a flame of

fire to be in to be at home with

the children to be in a perfect stillness.

2

To delight to delight those who are friends to

delight friends by turning by turning

in an enclosed space *in*

nape, which is napalm, or

which the military now likes to

refer to as incinder jell, as if

it were as harmless as Jello,

an after-dinner dessert. But it was napalm.

Carry torches, carry each other.

To delight friends by turning in napalm

to run to run in a circle

to be a light to be a light running

turning and running in a circle.

To delight to delight those who are friends to

delight friends by turning by turning

in a space *in nape, which is*

napalm, which the military

likes as incinder

jell after the fires burned down and

there was an old man lying on a cot, burned

to death with his hands stiff in rigor mortis.

Carry torches, carry each other.

To delight friends by turning burning hands in napalm

to run burning in a circle

to be a light running

and burning to death in a circle.

To delight to delight those who are friends to

delight friends by turning by turning

in nape, which is napalm, which the

military likes after the fires burned down and

there was an old man burned

to death with his hands stiff in

rigor mortis reaching

for the sky in prayer or supplication.

Carry torches, carry each other.

To delight friends by praying with hands in napalm

to run burning a

light burning to death in

a circle to be unable to help oneself.

To delight to delight those who are friends to

delight friends by turning

in nape, napalm, which the military

likes and there was an old man burned to

death with hands stiff in reaching

in prayer or supplication

forgiving us what we had done and

there was an old woman lying dead curled.

Carry torches, carry each other.

To delight friends praying with curled hands in napalm

to run a light running

burning to death to be unable to

help to find the river.

To delight to delight those who are *in nape*

napalm the military

likes and there was an old man with

hands stiff in prayer forgiving

what we had done and there was an old woman lying

dead curled into the fetal position

as if she had just been born an

old man lay beside her.

Carry torches, carry each other.

To delight friends with hands born curled in napalm

to run burning

to death to be unable

to help find the river unable to find water.

To delight to delight those *in nape napalm the*

military and there was an old man in

prayer forgiving

what we had done and there was an old woman lying

curled in the fetal position

as if she had just been born an old

man lay beside her and

there were thirty dead children.

Carry torches, carry each other.

To delight friends with children curled in napalm

to run to death to

be unable to find the river unable

to be a way to water.

To delight *in nape napalm and*

there was an old man forgiving

what we had done and there was an

old woman lying curled as

if she had just been born an old man lay beside

her and there were thirty dead children

now these kids, thirty of them, none were over

fifteen some of them were babies.

Carry torches, carry each other.

To delight friends with baby children in napalm

to run to death to

find the river water

to be unable to be a way to be a wave.

In nape napalm there was an old man forgiving   .

there was an old woman lying

as if she had just been born an old man

there were thirty dead children

none over fifteen some were babies

some looked like they had just been sunburned

their skins were a

very ruddy, ruddy pink or scarlet color.

Carry torches, carry each other.

To delight friends with babies scarlet in napalm

unable to find water

unable to conduct them on

the way on the way into a wave.

Napalm a forgiving old man napalm an

old woman lying as if

she had just been born an old man thirty dead children

napalm thirty dead babies

to look like they had just been sunburned

their skins a ruddy pink or

scarlet color napalm

napalm others charred with their guts hanging out.

Carry torches, carry each other.

To delight friends with babies charred in napalm

unable to plunge into

a wave able

to join with them joined together with the children.

3

To lift to lift up to lift without

effort to lift the head to

lift the head up without effort to remove the

cap cap of ashes to lift the head into

the air to remove the cap to

lift the head up

into the air without effort to

lift the head to sing sursum virga and sursum.

Carol heart's ease ring of flower's thought.

To lift the head up without

effort to sing without effort to hold hands with

men and women to sing and

hold hands with the children as a chorus.

To lift to lift up to lift without

effort to lift the head up

without effort to remove the cap of ashes

to lift the head into

air without effort to lift the

head to sing sursum virga

to sing sursum to sing coming forth coming

from the house to go singing past the doorkeeper.

Carol heart's ease ring of flower's thought.

To lift up to go singing

to hold hands with men and women

to sing and hold hands with the children

to go forward as a chorus without burden.

To lift to lift up to lift without

effort to lift the head up to remove the

cap of ashes to lift into air to

sing sursum virga sursum

to sing coming forth from the house to

go singing not rush to

go singing past the doorkeeper

to lead bones out of napalm out of confusion.

Carol heart's ease ring of flower's thought.

To lift up out of confusion to go singing

to hold hands to

go forward as a chorus without

burden without broken backs without bridles.

To lift to lift up to lift without

effort to lift the head up to remove ashes

to sing sursum virga sursum

to sing coming forth from the house to

go singing past the doorkeeper

to lead bones out of

napalm out of confusion

to be capable of motion of dance-with-song motion.

Carol heart's ease ring of flower's thought.

To lift up out of confusion by dancing in song motion

to go as a chorus

unburdened unbridled

to dance to permutations of bells.

To lift to lift up to lift without

effort to lift the head to

move ashes to sing sursum virga and sursum

coming from the house past the doorkeeper

to lead bones to be capable

of motion of dance-with-song motion

to go dancing and singing

in motion with bones with no ghost tones.

Carol heart's ease ring of flower's thought.

To lift up bones by dancing by singing in motion

to go as an unburdened chorus

as the morning

stars to the permutations of bells.

To lift to lift up to lift without

effort to lift the

head to move ashes to sing sursum and virga

from house past doorkeeper

to sing sursum to lead bones to be capable

of dance-with-song motion

to go dancing and singing with bones with no ghost tones

to wait no longer to go dancing.

Carol heart's ease ring of flower's thought.

To lift up bones to go dancing as a dancing

chorus as the morning

stars to permutations of

cowbells and tubular bells of gongs and tam-tams.

To lift to lift up to lift without

effort to lift the head to sing sursum

past the doorkeeper

to sing virga sursum to lead bones in motion

dance-with-song motion

dancing and singing with no ghost bones

to wait no longer for a coming hour to wait no

longer for the giving of new names.

Carol heart's ease ring of flower's thought.

To lift up bones with new names to go dancing

as a chorus of morning stars to

bells to cowbells and tam-tams

to trust in the striking of the gongs.

To lift to lift up to lift without

effort to lift to sing sursum sursum

to sing virga to lead in dance-with-song motion

dancing and singing with ghostless bones

to wait to wait no longer

for a coming hour to give new names

dancing and singing into

the river valley between blue mountains.

Carol heart's ease ring of flower's thought.

To lift up bones to dance into the river valley

as morning star chorus

to go dancing in perfect time

to trust in the striking of the gongs.

To lift to lift up to lift without

effort to sing sursum sursum virga

to lead dance-with-song motion with bones

to wait no longer

for a coming hour to give new names to

lead dancing and singing bones

into the river valley between blue mountains

into my city streets of my city.

Carol heart's ease ring of flower's thought.

To lift up bones to dance in the streets

to go dancing in perfect time

to trust in the striking of gongs

to go dancing in the streets of my city.

To lift to lift up to lift without

effort to sing sursum sursum

and humiliter sing lower

to lead dance-with-song motion with bones

to lead dancing and singing

bones into the streets of my city

bones wearing crowns wearing crowns of

mirrors crowns of mirrors on which the night wind blows.

Carol heart's ease ring of flower's thought.

To lift up bones on which the night wind blows

to go dancing in the streets in

perfect time to count steps to dance low

to sing low back and forth to sing low.

To lift to lift up to lift without

effort to sing humiliter

sing lower to lead dance-with-song motion

to lead bones dancing singing into

the streets of my city

bones wearing crowns of mirrors

on which the night wind blows bones wearing

crowns and harnesses of bells harnesses of tiny bells.

Carol heart's ease ring of flower's thought.

To lift up bones wearing mirror crowns and

harnesses of bells six hundred

tiny bells to dance low

with tiny bells to sing low back and forth with bells.

To lift to lift up to lift without

effort to sing humiliter

sing lower to sing podatus

to lead bones dancing into the streets of my city

bones wearing crowns of mirrors

and harnesses of bells like cicadas

to lead to count steps to dance low to

count steps to bow to count to salute.

Carol heart's ease ring of flower's thought.

To lift up bones which bow low and salute

which bow and salute which bow and salute

in harnesses of tiny bells

which sing back and forth singing *sana*.

To lift to lift up to lift without

effort to sing humiliter humiliter

to be the skeleton leader

to lead bones dancing into the

streets wearing crowns of mirrors and harnesses

of bells like cicadas

to lead to count steps to bow to

lead bones over railroad tracks to the square.

Carol heart's ease ring of flower's thought.

To lift up bones over railroad tracks

bones which bow and salute which bow and salute

in harnesses of bells

which sing back and forth singing *sana ta*.

To lift to lift up to lift without

effort to sing humiliter podatus humiliter

to lead bones into the streets wearing

crowns of mirrors and cicadas

to count steps to bow and salute

over railroad tracks

to lead bones singing *sana tafan*

into the square under the bank's clock.

Carol heart's ease ring of flower's thought.

To lift up bones under the bank's clock

bones which bow and salute

salute with hands flat down with elbows out

which sing back and forth *sana tafan tana.*

To lift to lift up to lift without

effort to sing humiliter and podatus

to lead bones wearing crowns of mirrors

bones that are crackling rays

to bow and salute over railroad tracks to

lead bones singing *sana tafan tana*

in the square bowing

and singing *sana tafan tana tan.*

Carol heart's ease ring of flower's thought.

To lift up bones singing *sana tafan*

bones which bow and salute

bowing with hands flat down with elbows out

singing *sana tafan tana tanaf.*

To lift to lift up to lift without

effort to sing humiliter podatus

to lead bones that are rays that crackle

and hum in the night wind

to bow and salute as if advancing to thrones

to lead rays singing

sana tafan tana between

traffic lights *sana tafan tana tanaf tam.*

Carol heart's ease ring of flower's thought.

To lift up bones that are singing lights singing

tafan tana tanaf

bowing as if advancing to thrones

sana tafan tana tanaf tamafts.

To lift to lift up to lift without

effort to sing podatus

to lead crackling and humming rays to

bow and salute as if advancing to thrones on

invisible ways of conveyance

to lead rays in singing

sana tafan tana tanaf

singing *sana tafan tana tanaf tamafts.*

Carol heart's ease ring of flower's thought.

To lift up bones that are singing *tana*

tana tanaf that bow and

sing *sana tafan*

advancing *sana tafan tana tanaf tamafts bai.*

To lift to lift up to lift without

effort to sing podatus again podatus

to lead rays to bow and

salute as if advancing to thrones in the dance with

songs of healing

to lead rays in singing *sana*

sana tafan singing the whole song *sana*

tafan tana tanaf tamafts bai.

Carol heart's ease ring of flower's thought.

To lift up bones singing the whole song

sana tafan tana tanaf tamafts bai

bones singing the whole song

sana tafan tana tanaf tamafts bai.

To lift to lift up to lift without

effort to sing tene

to relax the circling rays to

stand still that the citizens of my city

may be drawn as with visible

chains to this splendor splendor of coronation

that they may see the shape of

the dance that they may see the lily-flower.

Carol heart's ease ring of flower's thought.

To lift up bones in the lily-flower dance

in the flower's leaf ranged around

leaf splendid

bones as leaves and petals curled around each other.

To lift to lift up to lift without

effort to sing tene

to hold tene to relax the circle of rays

that the citizens of my city

may be drawn as with chains to splendor

that they may see the shape of

the dance see all the counsel and all the

perfection of the lily-flower.

Carol heart's ease ring of flower's thought.

To lift up bones in the perfection of the flower

in the leaf around flower leaf

splendid bones as

leaves and petals curled around each other.

To lift to lift up to lift without

effort to sing tene tene

to relax the circle that the citizens

may be drawn as with chains as

a man is drawn to his beloved object

drawn to splendor

of the dance to the counsel

the perfection and commodity of the lily-flower.

Carol heart's ease ring of flower's thought.

To lift up bones in the commodity of the flower

leaf around leaf perfection

splendid bones as

leaves and petals curled around each other.

To lift to lift up to lift without

effort to sing tene and auge

to draw as with chains as to the beloved

object as the curious

are drawn by the noise of miracle

to draw to the dance

to the counsel the perfection

the commodity and desire of the lily-flower.

Carol heart's ease ring of flower's thought.

To lift up bones in the desire of the flower

in the profuse but perfect

desire of bones as

leaves and petals in-curled around each other.

To lift to lift up to lift without

effort to sing tene to sing auge

to draw to the beloved object as the curious

to miracle as the

pitiful are drawn to woeful spectacle

to draw to the dance

the counsel perfection

commodity and desire of the lily-flower.

Carol heart's ease ring of flower's thought.

To lift up bones in the counsel of the flower

perfect and irresistible

counsel of bones as

leaves and petals curled around each other.

To lift to lift up to lift without

effort to sing tene auge

to draw to the object as the curious to miracle

the pitiful to spectacle the

ill to distribution of the cure

to draw to the dance

counsel perfection

commodity desire of the lily-flower.

Carol heart's ease ring of flower's thought.

To lift up bones in the whole of the flower

irresistible and glorious

whole made of bones as

leaves and petals curled around each other.

To lift to lift up to lift without

effort to sing high and low high and low

to hold to lengthen the singing of the carol

singing *sana sana tafan tana*

to sing the carol to stand still in the shining

dance in the lily-flower

in the ring of the flower's thought

in the light of day.

Carol heart's ease ring of flower's thought.

To lift up bones in light in curled leaves and petals

to intend the greatest gifts

to hold the shining

ring that is an ardor and a blossoming.

To lift to lift up to lift without

effort to sing high and low high and low

to hold and to lengthen the carol

singing *sana tafan tana tamaf*

to sing *tamaf tamafts* to stand still in the shining

dance in the lily-flower

in the ring of the flower's thought

in the light of day.

Carol heart's ease ring of flower's thought.

To lift bones up in light in curled leaves and petals

to intend the greatest gifts

to hold the shining

ring that is an ardor and a blossoming.

To lift to lift up to lift without

effort to sing high and low high and low

to hold and to lengthen the carol

sana tafan tana tamaf tamafts bai

sing *tamaf tamafts bai* to stand still in the shining

dance in the lily-flower

in the ring of the flower's thought

in the light of day.

Carol heart's ease ring of flower's thought.

To lift up bones in light in curled leaves and petals

to intend the greatest gifts

to hold the shining

ring that is an ardor and a blossoming.

Loop

1991

Sumac

for George Oppen

Freeze-dried, shrunk, crimson

plush crimped, thumbnail proof,

clothed with acid before rain.

One daughter answers beads,

the other flames, anything hot.

Current of pyramids crimson pyramids restless current

in which seeds are thrown syllables of other voices

within this motion as of monuments syllables to awaken

awaken hearts as risen flowers to rise up rise hearts

current of pyramids crimson pyramids restless current.

Current of pyramids crimson pyramids restless current

in which light-entered kings take shoulders for thrones

enthroned like boys riding the shoulders of blind men

drowned kings rise to a new music arise to guide men

current of pyramids crimson pyramids restless current.

Current of pyramids crimson pyramids restless current

in which stars drawn as starfish throng a changeable grid

stars drawn up to beads that return flame-beaded crowns

another answer crowns of love so many crowns of love

current of pyramids crimson pyramids restless current.

Babble Babble

Ba   ba   ba   ba
     bab   bab   bab   bab
babble   babble   babble   babble

like the solitary child who has no radio who
has no knowledge of how to turn the dial who would not know
how who would not know how constant song is in the air.

Ba   ba   ba   ba
     bab   bab   bab   bab
babble   babble   babble   babble

like the solitary child who has no radio who
has no knowledge of how to move on up a little higher
who would not know how to march all around the altar.

Ba   ba   ba   ba
     bab   bab   bab   bab
babble   babble   babble   babble

like the solitary child who has no radio who
has no knowledge of how it will always be howdy-howdy
howdy-howdy and never good-bye who would not know.

"Beware"

"Beware" wrote the famous Nicholas of Cusa

and I repeat his word to those who hear

who heard the call of that other word

constant call of that word and child on fire

who heard and smothered the word and child.

Beware of riverbeds into a chemical desert

sediment after rain gully after gully

singing bones won't be found among the gullies

dancing bones won't be found in the shadows

no shadows in true night of the true desert.

Beware of hope the hope of kingdom to come

you are already bones through whom words sing

all the words if one word is smothered

word is smothered if words aren't hoarded

stand against the crows ourselves as crows.

The Lily Alone

for Susan Howe

Alone lily alone the lily alone looks pantherine

look at the lily at bones as leaves and petals

bones as the ring bones as the ring of the flower

ring of the flower's thought the ring in motion

the motion of the ring is the motion of the animal

skin and muscles burned away the eyes burned also

burned to the essential to bone dance bone song

breath of song like the panther's fragrant breath

listen to the bones they have made your name sweet.

Were You

notes & a poem for Michael Palmer

When I began writing some notes for a poetics essay, in response to an invitation from Michael Palmer, there was no thought of turning them into a poem. What happened, however, is that the notes proposed a new poem, one that seemed to satisfy a lack in this collection. You could say the poem meant the demise of the essay. In fact, as I became more involved in the poem's composition, the notes were increasingly taken up with "practical" considerations until they disappeared altogether. The poem ate them up. Perhaps, then, the central principle of any poetics is that it ought to result in poetry. If nothing else, this should moderate the production of poetics essays.

If of interest, the Chernoff book referred to in the notes is *African Rhythm and African Sensibility* (Chicago, 1979), by John Miller Chernoff. The Messiaen poem is my own "That This May Be" (*New World Journal:* Summer, 1980). Caputo is John Caputo, author of *The Mystical Element in Heidegger's Thought* (Ohio, 1978). Spanos is William V. Spanos, editor of *Boundary 2;* his essay is "The Errant Art of Herman Melville: A Destructive Reading of *Moby Dick*," later published in his *The Errant Art of Moby-Dick* (Duke, 1995).

12.31.82

Primary: that the presumed goal of community is wrong and probably cannot be attained. The latter because individual vision challenges what has previously existed as a factor (agreed-upon image) for unity. Individual vision, when first presented, must be perceived as a threat, actually as something promoting disunity. It's remarkable that Blake continues to act in this way and will no doubt do so into the future. Could a church be organized around Blake?? His vision is too various.

An instance of community is gospel singing. One has to be struck by its power, vibrant out-reaching power and possibility for total involvement. The idea of critical detachment at a gospel service is anomalous. One either joins in or leaves; that's the choice.

The gospel service can't exist without complete prior agreement about the nature of the image/vision and its truthfulness. You can't doubt and sing with abandon. The identification, the location of the singer within the image has to be total. There is no room for the distance of irony.

The poem which establishes community will have to agree, in part, with the language of the old vision. Otherwise, the terms wouldn't be recognizable in any available, present way to an audience.

Am I thinking in terms of too simplistic an opposition in presuming the (new) poem must somehow destroy the old?

This isn't the right question.

There are things to do together and things to do by ourselves. Projects would be decided by scale. Language is not a project. By definition, it requires at least two interiors. Is anything improved when that number is increased? Perhaps the idea of one speaker and an audience of several auditors only apparently violates the nature of language as exchange.

Throw out the idea of money. The full house is still attractive. The larger the audience the more refined in the sense of simplifying the response. The larger the audience the less the possibility of involvement of individual members of the audience unless they confine themselves to the larger, single wave or direction of single mass response.

If there's to be, ultimately, destruction, then the beginning must offer the appearance of unified (recognizable) vision. How this can be done: by a fiction (several people are shown to sing together), by the use of terms that are evocative of past visions.

1.2.83

One way to have the poem fail: the audience is encouraged to be active (out loud) in its response and then is deliberately confused by the poet. The successful close of the poem is confusion. The poet has to retire in ignominy (but in secret triumph).

Poem as gospel service, poem as James Brown.

There should be some statement against performance poetry per se, that—in terms of traditional (tried, actually shared & practiced) ritual, especially by nonironic, nonwhite groups—it is so trivial, so merely aesthetic. The borrowing of Eno & David Byrne. These should be condemned.

What about the "spirituals" of Coltrane?

Write in the glisses, the sighs, the humming.

Artaud? Important, per Blake, that traditional terms be used. What one wants is such terms with utterly personal (private, untraditional) definitions; e.g., Jesus = the imagination.

There is a place for silence in a poetics. It's the desirable end goal.

Spanos is right to point out Melville's superiority to the Anti-Book, Anti-Scripture, the Satanism of the Romantics. The real test is whether one can stay quiet. Otherwise, each new poem is another mark of failure.

1.5.83

Yesterday, coming back from a walk with Sam, early evening, the sky divided toward the south in zones of color: bottom deep orange with outline of trees; above the orange as it starts to become pale a very light but intense violet; above that the light blue just before nightfall.

Looking back at my notes from Chernoff, I'm reminded that my assumption that a community, by definition, must be univocal isn't necessary. The community can be a "diversified assembly." The problem is how to make a separate contribution. Should it (can it) stay separate?

1.6.83

That is, separate & together.

first-phrase = (seed of) the pattern = several phrases or sentences; the standard pattern is repeated several times

dance to come out of a trance, to join a diversified assembly with a separate contribution

music & dance: ways of posing structures and restrictions for "ethical actualization"

power of the music lies in silence of the gaps; this is where one's contribution must go & by it the music may be opened up further. The idea is to conceive the music as an arrangement or system of gaps and not as a dense pattern of sound. This rules out Xenakis. What about Riley, Glass & Reich?

Say the rhythm before you play it. It may not be necessary to express this in nonsense syllables. Perhaps there could be such syllables which coalesce into words as the poem moves along.

Seed pattern: begin with a full phrase or sentence of words, then decompose it to syllables.

New poem should go in collection to break up the finale quality of the last two poems. This one needs to open the conclusion, air out, make for a new kind of silence (in, within the poem vs. "stunned" audience). The opening can be combined with the idea of deliberate (designed) failure. Go beyond Eno, that sort of borrowing. James White & the Blacks.

Consider relation of the four parts to gospel song, to the "story" of the broken glass from the signal which means the train won't come on time, may collide with another train, or may not come at all. Forget the red sky, it's too pretty. The opening seed pattern has to be a song of *result*, the state of affairs after the lens has been broken.

Interpolated: put full statements by way of commentary; i.e., this is the condition (landscape) that obtains *after* the destruction of the lens. The statements shouldn't be put in a section by themselves, but mixed, perhaps with the nonsense syllables.

I'll free you from demons, not capitalism!

think about it
repeats on the ends of phrases

Take end—work it out, elaborate it (into syllables, becoming more & more abstract, going toward pure gesture) and then return to extension of phrase given as words.

Ragged male voice shouting half-phrases, calm female choir *smoothly* singing whole phrases or sentences behind him.

God has done great things for me (Colossians)
run jump sing & shout

drop piano, organ, bass—expose voices then slowly—fairly soft—bring them back; end comes on only slightly higher tone, which is not really close to the intensity of the middle just before the instruments drop out.

slow, restrained scream

1.8.83

The music is organized to be open to the rhythmic interpretation anyone present wishes to contribute. This organization of openness is achieved by the gaps. One makes one's contribution—a new, additional rhythm—*in* the gaps.

I may be wrong in feeling antagonistic to Peter Gabriel, reaction of the obscure against the famous. Still, I doubt if the hybrid is all that desirable. The goal still remains transformation. It's plagiarism or worse if that doesn't happen. Not to reproduce a sound, then, but to use it as a general principle to make another sound.

The train: voice, agent of the voice, the word.

1.9.83

train won't deliver burning Dalí baby
no Vietnamese doll baby

Opening phrase: talk about the train
time for train talk   a rap??
the student said that just isn't an ordinary train
violet (why violet)   did you expect blue?

rumble of the trains, vibration
the vocal tract (larynx, pharynx, mouth) = resonant chamber

voice organ consists of: power supply

oscillator

resonator

The cycle of opening & closing—vocal cords acting like vibrating lips—feeds a train of air pulses (beating of the veins) into the vocal tract. The train of pulses produces a rapidly oscillating air pressure (throbbing, dilations) in the vocal tract—a sound.

The sound chopped by the vibrating vocal folds & generated by the airstream is the voice source. It is the raw material for speech or song. It is a complex tone composed of a fundamental frequency & a large number of overtones.

Messiaen identifies mode no. 2 with violet.

Complexes of resonances replace the concept of chords.

1.10.83

& I await the resurrection of the dead?

dehisce   (to yawn)

to open spontaneously when ripe

opening of (fruit) capsule by valves, slits or pores

splitting into definite parts

einöde   das Westgerm

poverty, want, give oneself away

jewel   heimat as home (not heaven), homeland

Ezekiel: the voice of the Almighty, the voice of speech

a voice that was over their heads

don't fall on your face/no voice

These never unravel their own intricacies, & have no proper endings; but as imperfect, unanticipated, & disappointing sequels (as mutilated stumps) hurry to abrupt intermergings—

That profound silence, that only voice of our God... from that divine thing without a name, those impostor philosophers pretend somehow to have got an answer; which is absurd, as though they should say they had got water out of stone; for how can a man get a Voice out of Silence?

1.11.83

The room (finite, resonant chamber) opens out onto the desert. One side or wall *is* the desert.

pt. 1 of poem = a)   train through the summer night, alone in a
              room, violet tongue (get rid of?), a wave,
              & Ezekiel (voice & sapphire throne)
        b)   desert   blood dried to dull brown (perhaps
              have terms of brilliance, but all put in ne-
              gation, canceled use   hymn tune
        a)   train

In a system of multirhythms—to keep your step—you have to hear the beat that is never sounded (hidden).

rule of repeats   repetition reveals depth of structure
                       (should be more, as *immediate,* in b)

fiction of audience supplying a beat to which I respond, use as basis for elaboration

the gaps: where & how big?
                    (never at same place on successive lines)

Looking at the last paintings ('68–70) Rothko did, I'm tempted to
stop. Shouldn't the poem—which may be the last one in the col-
lection—be grey, not red or violet?

The gaps in the first section of pt. 1 don't seem right. They're at
different places on the line, but feel arbitrary. Why should they
all be five spaces?

Good rhythm fills a gap in the other rhythms and creates an emp-
tiness that may be similarly filled.

Adapting Chernoff, the open quality of the rhythm becomes a
deception; if the call isn't actual, then the response must be stran-
gled. A deceptive call to strangle the response. The organization
should *look* open.

So: first pt. appears open, to invite response
        second is oblivious, completely closed

        3rd returns to acknowledge, in terms of 1, that the
        possibilities are good (same words, different tone)
        or that the very same calls are made in this final
        pt., but they're given without hope. Problem of in-
        tonation (on the page).

Re Caputo's comparison (Heidegger & Meister E): an experience
with language can lead out, does lead out into "the world."

Term in his letter: *wiederholung*   retrieval of what somehow
                                        gets said in the work, not
                                        necessarily what its author
                                        intended

The difficulty isn't in the cancellation, but in providing something after the x-out. I think this will have to show up in the second pt. This won't alter what comes in the third, i.e., disillusioned repeat or near repeat of pt. 1.

perhaps mention the poem is a late thought, something unexpected, added on to the collection

1.14.83

Time to consider what should go in the middle section of ten lines. One thing: it must be continually dense, very tight rhythm.

Think about feeding the Rothko quote (when red does appear, it is like a flame of self-immolation) throughout.

The idea of dried blood as the dominant color, color of the desert.

This is *after* the train doesn't come.

You were waiting alone in a room for the train, in a resonant chamber. One side or wall of the room opens out to the desert. The room, in fact, is more a number of perspective lines than an actual construction of walls.

This section should be so dense that the reader or listener is immobilized, unable to move.

1.15.83

could begin with "were you"

That the section of 10 lines be "about" the closing up of the gaps, that gaps themselves—with perhaps some quotation from Chernoff—be a reference.

unresting

Or: leave first part as "fiction"; then the following overlays oper-
ate as commentary (gaps, Chernoff, the revisitation of the Mes-
siaen poem)

> explanation re lips, tongue
> that the bk. was supposed to be done

Went back to Spanos's essay last night. He argues that Ishmael,
contra Father Mapple, uses language interrogatively. Presumably
this connects with Heidegger's thinking-as-asking. He borrows
Derrida's process of supplementarity for this as a process of repe-
tition which always delays a final measuring—defers presence
& thus allows the thing to go on living. Thus mystery is kept or
enacted in an active way as opposed to the French always mouth-
ing off about mystère, etc.

A naming that's an interrogation of Naming? Does he mean a
questioning of the Word, provenance of His saying? One form
would be to doubt, but not *the doubter* per se, member of a sect
in itself. It seems possible that this is what occurs with the active
use—more than "use"—of metaphor. What separates it from the
New Yorker decorators is that it begins at the beginning of the
poem and continues, as a process, throughout. Not merely inci-
dental modification of the cast-iron noun structures (always false,
whatever the comfort). This may be connected with Ashbery.
When I say I want the poem to fail, it's in terms of offering that
assuring structure in new & winning ways. Now the interesting
thing is to appear to offer just such ways and still make the struc-
ture, hope for & claim of structure, fail.

Always erring *words,* not the original/abiding Word

Ishmael has a disaffiliative enterprise

> a carefull errancy. When Spanos says that seeming for
> Ishmael is always seeming, the statement affirms the function

of active metaphor. This way it's understood that poetry as the formal profession (?) of metaphor, will continue—forget the question of audience—because of the nature of metaphor itself (unresting), the end of any single poem or the volume of anyone's collected works no more than a pause, parenthesis that will have to be open-ended on the right-hand side.

per etymology of *Dia-bolos*, poet as scatterer, disseminator, dis-simulator—the finite, eccentric, dialogic voice that repeats & retrieves the *dia-spora*

to give undecidability a positive value (negative capability) to bear witness, to be a witness (this doesn't, contra Olson's empha-sis on the topological—as if everything happens in terms of space & surface—refer only to object and event)

There *is* the mind, theater of the mind.

un-name the beasts

tears at his clothes
keep throwing away, speed
up the decay process

1.16.83
Gk   ereuthein = to redden

at the least refracted end of the spectrum
color of blood, fire, poppy, rose & ripe fruits

sky at dawn or sunset
of the cheeks, lips
dyed with red   red flag
forget violet
You were

1.17.83

By chance saw the Tarahumara dancers on TV!

1.18.83

Idea for overlay—section 3, over the middle 10 lines—attack the embrace of the father, embrace of the soul by the father, at the end of B's Jerusalem. That this—after the picture is given—somehow won't happen, that the Word, contra E, won't be born.

Pulses make sound, and the sound becomes the Word. Perhaps use some of Ong's statements on the word as sound.

(For bottom overlay: note that the words—*were you ready,* etc.—are the same, but the tone's changed.)

1.22.83

lines like puffed sleeves

mention the fiction of the broken glass?

This is a dense pattern of sound & not a system of gaps

Melville: imperfect unanticipated disappointing sequels
              mutilated stumps hurry

Xenakis: a book of screens equals the life of a complex
              sound
              each screen is made up of cells of clouds of grains

no room inside for movement

Augustine on repetition: a mode of assuring the seeker that he is on his way, and is not merely wandering blindly through the chaos from which all form arises

the train carries & is the voice, is the Word

God speaks his word in the birth of the son

true language = a response to the Word which the Father addresses to us (response = letting the Father speak his Word *in* us)

all human language must be silenced before the Father speaks

verbum cordis, silent inner word

through song the singer & the listener become identical

Father's son/word is personal & *breath-given*

word is in speaker as seed in source

> the only source of flames
> whose tongue pierces and
> gathers the taste for the
> Word

(last section can deal with the question of whether there's anything left after the negation)

We don't have the promise of the next breath—Jerry Lee

1.23.83

Gloomy Sunday!

Decided to leave bottom of the first page as it is, a repeat of the opening. Yesterday I thought it would have to be changed in the interests of variety. But, as I come to see, this is an eye demand. When I speak the parts, they're different, i.e., the opening fairly brisk and aggressive, the close slower and tentative. The real question is whether there should be, as in music, reading notation or instructions of some sort included, put in the margin.

new poem: How to Read Me

section 3 = 13 lines   1 overlap from 2 & 2 lines in the space between

Ives was trying to protect a fading transcendentalism behind all the noise, no? *That's* the unanswered question.

1.24.83

What is the connection between the train — train time & being fed the train — and dancing in the gaps? Turned around, what's the connection between there being no gaps to dance in and the train's nonarrival?

In the top & bottom sections, there is the promise of the train to be fed inside by the tongue of the father. Granted, this is past tense. (Pages after the first should be in the present?) If the gaps are closed, there can't be a dance or only a confused attempt. If you can't dance, you can't join the assembly.

First 3 lines deal with the gaps; beginning with the 4th they modulate back to the train or allow some sort of show-through from the middle section.

Perhaps even those lines, the first 3, shouldn't refer to the gaps because the thrust of the second page is clear enough. But: have to keep the last one for the overlap. Their disposition would be completely different if the first of the 3 begins with something other than "if."

Joining the dance = getting on, being part of the train?
Just say no gaps no train.
1st line: carried over from 2 with some addition
2nd & 3rd: transition (gaps → train)
4–13: train (use Eck., possibly Ong)

1.26.83

Looks like the whole deal of there being no gaps—or that the gaps have been closed by the song in the air—will have to go in the last section as a series of questions.

2.6.83

"Were You" finished? Happy enough to type it up and clear off the desk of notes and the big cardboard sheets. Final section of 5 lines could go this way:

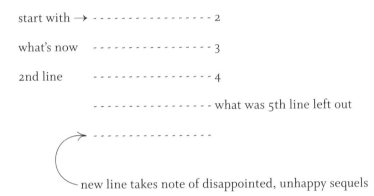

start with → - - - - - - - - - - - - - - - - 2

what's now   - - - - - - - - - - - - - - - - 3

2nd line   - - - - - - - - - - - - - - - - 4

              - - - - - - - - - - - - - - - - what was 5th line left out

              - - - - - - - - - - - - - - -

new line takes note of disappointed, unhappy sequels

But: may be wrong to want more of a da da dum end. Enough to pause a bit in reading the last line as it is. Let the past tense do the work. Important that the tone isn't too harsh; it shouldn't sound superior.

Were You

Were you ready   ready ready   ready for train time
           were you   were you
time to be fed   tongue   to feed train inside you
           were you   were you
train in   in waves of a as in father   amen train
      were you   were you

you were ready you were you were as you were as ready as you were
ready as you could be ready for ready for train time the violet
train you were as ready as ready for the love train "let's start a
love train" you were ready to pull the train ready as could be
to pull the train through the summer night "let's start" ready for
the end of the song "come on come on" ready for violet tongue to
tongue to feed violet train inside train in the train of pulses in
pulses inside you "come on come on" inside you in waves of a
waves of a as in father ready for the end for the father's tongue
you were ready for the father father's tongue to touch your teeth

were you ready   ready ready   ready for train time
           were you   were you
time to be fed   tongue   to feed train inside you
           were you   were you
train in   in waves of a as in father   amen train
      were you   were you.

Were you ready to place your foot in the gaps

were you ready to place confidence in the gaps

were you ready to enter a trance in the gaps.

Were you ready to enter a trance in the gaps were
you ready to do the locomotion in the silent gaps were you
ready to be entranced in the silence of the gaps ready
read-ee-ee-ee you were you were "could be ready for"
you were as ready as rain you were ready to pull
the train through the sum of the song "come on come
to feed violet train insid inside you "come on come o
fa as in father read-ee-ee-ee-ee-ee ready for father
to give the word train of pulses is a word ready to
be fed to be given the inside secret word *verbum cordis*
not say a word hushed to let father let father feed
feed give speak the word hushed in response soul's
language is hushed language of response you were ready.

Were you ready to listen and to understand in the gaps

were you ready to understand with a dance in the gaps

were you ready to do the dip with father in the gaps

were you ready to be embraced like Jerusalem in the gaps

were you ready to give birth to the word in the gaps.

Nativity

If you kneel

sender will teach

will teach you

here's a sender

no bright harness

still a sender

if you kneel

will teach you

teach the shout

sender says listen

listen to sender

sender number one

gle glo glory

that's the shout

if you kneel

sender in white

in greyblue shadows

will teach you.

Sender says listen

gle glo glory

that's the shout

the first shout

listen to sender

kneel and listen

sender number two

no bright harness

kneel down now

sender in lilac

will teach you

bleeding throat shout

the first shout

listen now listen

kneel and listen

sender with fiddle

fiddle without strings

will teach you.

That's the shout

sender number three

in lavender blue

typical heavenly color

will teach you

the first shout

gle glo glory

the bleeding shout

come kneel down

can't you kneel

no bright harness

kneel a little

come listen now

can't you listen

kneel and listen

the first shout

the third sender

will teach you.

From across the sea from across glass

gathered brought together are gathered

as in a mantle as bees in the crystal

gathered brought together by the word

from across the sea cross glass to die.

What glass sea of glass before crystal

who gathered all who hear are gathered

what crystal throne center threshold

what crystal where word is word is stilled

word embraced to die to enter the desert.

Word and child in a blue fire

word and child leap from throne

word and child run toward us.

What word word born unceasingly

what child child calling calling

who're we embracers smotherers.

Wandering no whining boys wandering bones back in the desert
in the desert again the desert with and without possibilities
without harping solemn choir without choir of angel senders
no senders will teach you in true night in true desert night
endless summer night no winter wild for bones away from light
away from the lighted highway from light-reflecting signs
bones play designless play all night long play with all words
play with all the words with the possibility of all the words
all words are possible for bones all for the singing of bones

      how enter the desert with and without possibilities
      how enter the endless summer night no winter wild

cross sea of glass to throne center threshold to the crystal
to crystal where the word where the child is born unceasingly
new-born word and child in blue fire word and child on fire
word and child on fire run toward us calling and calling us
hear the call embrace word and child we are the embracers
we embrace to smother cheek on cheek to smother to make still
still word and child made still cheek made to burn to bones
bones can cross through crystal we can cross to the desert
to all the words to all night long song with all the words.

What pleasure to move among bones in the endless summer night

what pleasure to be capable of motion dance-with-song motion

what pleasure to dance and sing all the words all night long.

Never Too Late

desan epistamenos, epaoide d' aima kelainon
ODYSSEY XIX, 457

1

One word two vowels one active situation at a time

desan is one word one situation one with two enactors

one situation of tying of binding of tying down

the meaning in vowels enacted meaning in the word meaning

in a long e in eta down in the fair and opened mouth

eta sex queen's vowel fair open mouth the bait

appearance of tits and ass tits and ass appear monstrous

fair mouth sings tea for two you for me ah you for me

in short a in alpha the lowest pitched even rough

alpha   =   moon   =   white light   =   white night-gown

never too late to reread the beautiful mythology of Greece

night-gown twists and twists around you in your sleep

not what was expected not the anticipated enactment

the enactment not anticipated in the situation

combed white heads of the enactors become deathless heads

deathless the dream women who are to be tied down.

2

One word three new vowels another active situation

epistamenos is one word one situation with three enactors

one situation of knowing how to tie dreams down

the meaning in vowels not anticipated in the situation

in short e in epsilon vowel of a new kind of monster

evolution of glitter-eyes the boy-god the thief

new monster sold wisdom for a coat of flames

will trade coat act of the faith that comes with the coat

in short i in iota lips made thin made unclarifying

unclear postcard of sunset skies retouched tinged

iota vowel of the great principle of light vowel of the gilder

would sunlight god decree winter in America wouldn't he

in long o in omega crow vowel crow's caw has an edge

old-style monster crow with hooked knife that's crow's bill

supposedly can be imprisoned in winter put him in prison

imprison him fetter him or get ready for combat.

3

One word diphthong two articulations in one syllable

two in one open alpha then glide in direction of iota

there's one active situation under all the others

one situation undercuts others the one situation of dying

aima is one word one situation with me the enactor

do I forget one other word one word before aima

epaoide situation of the new functional charm me the enactor

me to enact the new charm that cuts that opens the wound

bleed is the cry *let it bleed let it bleed*'s my cry

the resident power the life the life in common the house

let it let it bleed let it bleed over you all over me

if you need someone to *bleed* on *bleed* all over me

this is the new charm that cuts and opens the wound

new charm cuts new function not the old crow

we've been wounded by phantoms in a wide landscape of snow

cut and open the wound bleed on bleed on the snow.

4

One word vowel diphthong new vowel active situation

kelainon is one word one situation with ourselves enactors

one situation of black of black blood on snow

the meaning in the vowel enacts the meaning in the word

in short o in omicron the vowel of hurt personified

companions of hurt personification of curses

they lead the phantoms back phantoms on the blood-soul

combed white deathless heads new and old monsters

force and motion hunted down in a landscape of snow

this is in black and white this is a motion study

motion almost the same motion almost no motion

the same motion we're the raw heads we're the bloody bones

we are the raw heads connected to the bloody bones

ourselves the enactors of the last word the last situation

not what was expected abrupt nightfall on snow

in this night we wander through snow toward the desert.

Against the Nurses of Experience

The faces of the nurses are green and pale

green and pale faces call to the children

call the children to come home from play

there's no thread not a thread of the sun.

The voices of the children are bone voices

bones sing the song of all possible words

all words all through the night without end

we will never never come in we are at home.

Orange Berries Dark Green Leaves

Darkened not completely dark let us walk in the darkened field

trees in the field outlined against that which is less dark

under the trees are bushes with orange berries dark green leaves

not poetry's mixing of yellow light blue sky darker than that

darkness of the leaves a modulation of the accumulated darkness

orange of the berries another modulation spreading out toward us

it is like the reverberation of a bell rung three times

like the call of a voice the call of a voice that is not there.

We will not look up how they got their name in a book of names

we will not trace the name's root conjecture its first murmuring

the root of the berries their leaves is succoured by darkness

darkness like a large block of stone hauled on a wooden sled

like stone formed and reformed by a dark sea rolling in turmoil.

In True Night

Of the constant song I keep some of the words

some of the basic words of the song in the air

crystal is a basic word crystal not paradise

procession to the crystal to the child on fire

child the most basic word most haunting word

those who hear cross glass to embrace the child

child embraced to smother not to enter heaven

not heaven but the desert one more basic word

bones basic word enter desert basic word to dance

to dance lily-flower dance and forget the steps

to sing the song beyond all songs on the radio.

2

Night falls night fallen true night is fallen

true night truly most destitute time is fallen

destitute most destitute in the midnight hour

it is always the midnight hour in the desert

nothing in the desert to raise the hand against

night falls night fallen true night is fallen

there is nothing no gift to raise the hand for

no love to come no love to come tumbling down

love cannot begin to shine the star cannot

star cannot shine wise men can't find their way

night falls night fallen true night is fallen.

3

Night falls night fallen true night is fallen

true night basic word of the song in the air

crystal basic word crystal in the midnight hour

it is always the crystal hour in the desert

child in the desert child most haunting word

night falls night fallen true night is fallen

nothing there to smother to raise the hand for

no love to come love come one more basic word

bones begin to shine like stars in the dance

lily-flower shines wise men can't get the steps

night falls night fallen true night is fallen.

The Rothko Chapel Poem

Red deepened by black red made deep by black

prolation of deep red like stairs of lava

deep red like stairs of lava to gather us in

gather us before the movements are to be made

red stairs lead us lead us to three red rooms

rooms of deep red light red deepened by black

in this first room there is to be a wedding

we are the guests the welcome wedding guests

the groom welcomes us the bride welcomes us

rooms full of deep red light room upon room

in this second room there is to be a wedding

we are the guests the welcome wedding guests

the groom welcomes us the bride welcomes us

the bride and groom take our hands in welcome

room on room third room full of deep red light

in this third room there is to be a wedding

we are the guests the welcome wedding guests

the groom welcomes us the bride welcomes us

bride and groom take our hands in their hands.

Deepened by black red made deep by black

prolation of deep red like cooled lava

the stairs in a cooler prolation of red

there are still the movements to be made

stairs led us led us to three red rooms

rooms of cooled light red cooled by black

in the first room there was a wedding

we were guests we were the wedding guests

groom welcomed us and bride welcomed us

rooms full of cooled light room upon room

in the second room there was a wedding

we were guests we were the wedding guests

groom welcomed us and bride welcomed us

bride and groom took our hands in welcome

room upon room full of cooled red light

in the third room there was a wedding

we were guests we were the wedding guests

groom welcomed us and bride welcomed us

bride and groom took our hands in theirs.

Bride and groom took our hands in theirs

groom welcomed us and bride welcomed us

we were guests we were the wedding guests

in the third room there was a wedding

room upon room full of cooled red light

bride and groom took our hands in welcome

groom welcomed us and bride welcomed us

we were guests we were the wedding guests

in the second room there was a wedding

rooms full of cooled light room upon room

groom welcomed us and bride welcomed us

we were guests we were the wedding guests

in the first room there was a wedding

rooms of cooled light red cooled by black

stairs led us led us to three red rooms

there are still the movements to be made

the stairs in a cooler prolation of red

prolation of deep red like cooled lava

deepened by black red made deep by black.

Time for some passion in this language it's time to move

it's time to move to make a move ma—mah—moo-euve-veh

move out of deep red light move out of this purple light

the first movement is the movement of infinite resignation

did you think we would move together move as a gathering

did you think it'd be let's waltz come let's waltz time

it's time to make a move that ma—mah—moo-euve-veh time

move out of this purple light make the move by yourself

first movement of infinite resignation by yourself alone

did you think we'd move as a gathering of wedding guests

did you think it'd be let's waltz like wedding guests time

time for some passion in this language time to move alone

it's time to ma—mah—moo-euve-veh move alone move away

away by yourself away from deep red from this purple light

movement of resignation alone and away from the weddings

did you think we'd move as wedding guests hand in hand

did you think we'd waltz hand in hand with bride and groom

it's that ma—mah—moo-euve-veh time no other move time

always time for that time alone and away from warm welcome

resignation move away from warm welcome of bride and groom

did you think bride and groom wouldn't blacken their hands

did you think their hands wouldn't be as blackened to us

time for some passion time to move into black black rooms.

Time for some passion time to move into black black rooms

did you think their hands wouldn't be as blackened to us

did you think bride and groom wouldn't blacken their hands

resignation move away from warm welcome of bride and groom

always time for that time alone and away from warm welcome

it's that ma—mah—moo-euve-veh time no other move time

did you think we'd waltz hand in hand with bride and groom

did you think we'd move as wedding guests hand in hand

movement of resignation alone and away from the weddings

away by yourself away from deep red from this purple light

it's time to ma—mah—moo-euve-veh move alone move away

time for some passion in this language time to move alone

did you think it'd be let's waltz like wedding guests time

did you think we'd move as a gathering of wedding guests

first movement of infinite resignation by yourself alone

move out of this purple light make the move by yourself

it's time to make a move that ma—mah—moo-euve-veh time

did you think it'd be let's waltz come let's waltz time

did you think we would move together move as a gathering

the first movement is the movement of infinite resignation

move out of deep red light move out of this purple light

it's time to move to make a move ma—mah—moo-euve-veh

time for some passion in this language it's time to move.

Doorway without a door

shadow-crossed doorway

the doorway always open

one at a time inside

inside one hears screams

begins to hear screaming

screams within screams

screams in collision

turbulence of collision

turbulence in the rooms

screams in black rooms.

It is really only one scream

echoes of only one scream in

of one scream within itself

screams within the one scream

within one passionate scream

one scream has been sustained

one scream is being sustained

sustained in one black room

echoes of only one scream in

of one scream within itself

screams within the one scream

the one scream will not decay

not decay in one black room.

Not decay in one black room

the one scream will not decay

screams within the one scream

of one scream within itself

echoes of only one scream in

sustained in one black room

one scream is being sustained

one scream has been sustained

within one passionate scream

screams within the one scream

of one scream within itself

echoes of only one scream in

it is really only one scream.

One scream the motive for movement

movement from one room to another

from one black room into another

into this red room red after black

no red deeper than red after black

one scream the motive for movement

through black through empty rooms

feels like we're wandering through

through a seething and writhing sea

through black through black to red

one scream the motive for movement

movement from one room to another

from one black room into another

into this red room red after black

no red deeper than red after black.

Doorway without a door

shadow-crossed doorway

the doorway always open

one at a time inside

inside one hears screams

begins to hear screaming

screams within screams

screams in collision

turbulence of collision

turbulence in the rooms

screams in black rooms.

Only one scream really it is

only one scream within echoes

itself within the one scream

the one scream within screams

one passionate scream within

been sustained one scream has

being sustained one scream is

in one black room sustained

only one scream within echoes

itself within the one scream

the one scream within screams

will not decay in one scream

in one black room it will not.

In one black room it will not

will not decay in one scream

the one scream within screams

itself within the one scream

only one scream within echoes

in one black room sustained

being sustained one scream is

been sustained one scream has

one passionate scream within

the one scream within screams

itself within the one scream

only one scream within echoes

only one scream really it is.

No red deeper than red after black

into this red room red after black

from one black room into another

movement from one room to another

one scream the motive for movement

through black through black to red

through a seething and writhing sea

feels like we're wandering through

through black through empty rooms

one scream the motive for movement

no red deeper than red after black

into this red room red after black

from one black room into another

movement from one room to another

one scream the motive for movement.

Really only one has been moving us

only one within itself moving us

one scream within itself moving us

screams within the one move us away

away from the weddings wedding rooms

from those to this this black room

to our wandering in this black room

moving in this room means wandering

wandering's moving without meaning

no end to moving in this black room

it is like moving in a writhing sea

we are wandering in a writhing sea

seething and writhing in this room.

Seething and writing in this room

we are wandering in a writing sea

it is like moving in a writing sea

no end to moving in this black room

wandering's moving without meaning

moving in this room means wandering

to our wandering in this black room

from those to this this black room

away from the weddings wedding rooms

screams within the one move us away

one scream within itself moving us

only one within itself moving us

really only one has been moving us.

One scream the motive for wandering movement

movement in one black room in one in another

movement in a writhing sea in black rooms

movement into this red room red after black

no red goes deeper than this red after black

one scream the motive for wandering movement

scream from one child who's given one picture

one picture of blood this room full of blood

scream from one child given only one picture

the one child is the poet the child of pain

one scream the motive for wandering movement

movement in one black room in one in another

movement in a writhing sea in black rooms

movement into this red room red after black

no red goes deeper than this red after black.

Doorway without a door

the doorway always open

one at a time inside

one at a time I am one

no third person is one

one is I one is I me

the one primitive I me

I me the child of pain

the primitive I inside

inside the turbulence

inside the black rooms.

One I know really one scream

hard not to within one scream

what it is what the movement

same passionate same movement

first movement of resignation

same as before the same alone

away from the weddings alone

not in the wedding pictures

other other possible pictures

blacktop other blacktopped

not in other I me within one

echoes of in one black room

within one in one black room.

Within one in one black room

echoes of in one black room

not in other I me within one

blacktop other blacktopped

other other possible pictures

not in the wedding pictures

away from the weddings alone

same as before the same alone

first movement of resignation

same passionate same movement

what it is what the movement

hard not to within one scream

one I know really one scream.

The motive for movement one scream

from one room to another movement

into another from one black room

red after black into this red room

red after black no red deeper than

the motive for movement one scream

through empty rooms through black

wandering to music played backwards

seething writhing sea through it

through black to red through black

the motive for movement one scream

from one room to another movement

into another from one black room

red after black into this red room

red after black no red deeper than.

Doorway without a door

the doorway always open

one at a time inside

one at a time I am one

no third person is one

one is I one is I me

the one primitive I me

I me the child of pain

the primitive I inside

inside the turbulence

inside the black rooms.

One scream I know really one

one scream within hard not to

what the movement what it is

same movement same passionate

resignation's first movement

the same alone same as before

alone away from the weddings

wedding pictures not in the

possible pictures other other

blacktopped blacktop other

I me within me not in other

in one black room echoes of

in one black room within one.

In one black room within one

in one black room echoes of

I me within me not in other

blacktopped blacktop other

possible pictures other other

wedding pictures not in the

alone away from the weddings

the same alone same as before

resignation's first movement

same movement same passionate

what the movement what it is

one scream within hard not to

one scream I know really one.

Red after black no red deeper than

red after black into this red room

into another from one black room

from one room to another movement

the motive for movement one scream

through black to red through black

seething writhing sea through it

wandering to music played backwards

through empty rooms through black

the motive for movement one scream

red after black no red deeper than

red after black into this red room

into another from one black room

from one room to another movement

the motive for movement one scream.

Been moving me really only one had

moving me only one within itself

moving me one scream within itself

move me away screams within the one

wedding rooms away from the weddings

this black room from those to this

this black room I'm wandering in this

wandering means moving in this room

moving without meaning's wandering

in this black room no end to moving

a writhing sea like moving in a sea

in a writhing sea I am wandering

in this room seething and writhing.

In this room seething and writhing

in a writing sea I am wandering

a writing sea like moving in a sea

in this black room no end to moving

moving without meaning's wandering

wandering means moving in this room

this black room I'm wandering in this

this black room from those to this

wedding rooms away from the weddings

move me away screams within the one

moving me one scream within itself

moving me only one within itself

been moving me really only one has.

No red goes deeper than this red after black

movement into this red room red after black

movement in a writhing sea in black rooms

movement in one black room in one in another

one scream the motive for wandering movement

the one child is the poet the child of pain

scream from one child given only one picture

one picture of blood this room full of blood

scream from one child who's given one picture

one scream the motive for wandering movement

no red goes deeper than this red after black

movement into this red room red after black

movement in a writhing sea in black rooms

movement in one black room in one in another

one scream the motive for wandering movement.

It's time to move time for some passion in this language

to make a move ma—mah—moo-euve-veh it's time to move

move out of this purple light move out of deep red light

the second movement is the movement of rosy transparency

move as a gathering did you think we would move together

come let's waltz time did you think it'd be let's waltz

that ma—mah—moo-euve-veh time it's time to make a move

make the move by yourself move out of this purple light

by yourself alone second movement of rosy transparency

as wedding guests did you think we'd move as a gathering

like wedding guests did you think it'd be let's waltz time

time to move alone time for some passion in this language

move alone move away it's time to ma—mah—moo-euve-veh

away from deep red from this purple light away by yourself

alone and away from the weddings movement of transparency

hand in hand did you think we'd move as wedding guests

hand in hand with bride and groom did you think we'd waltz

no other move time it's that ma—mah—moo-euve-veh time

alone and away from warm welcome always time for that time

away from warm welcome of bride and groom transparency move

blacken their hands did you think bride and groom wouldn't

as blackened to us did you think their hands wouldn't be

time to move into black black rooms time for some passion.

Time to move into black black rooms time for some passion

as blackened to us did you think their hands wouldn't be

blacken their hands did you think bride and groom wouldn't

away from warm welcome of bride and groom transparency move

alone and away from warm welcome always time for that time

no other move time it's that ma—mah—moo-euve-veh time

hand in hand with bride and groom did you think we'd waltz

hand in hand did you think we'd move as wedding guests

alone and away from the weddings movement of transparency

away from deep red from this purple light away by yourself

move alone move away it's time to ma—mah—moo-euve-veh

time to move alone time for some passion in this language

like wedding guests did you think it'd be let's waltz time

as wedding guests did you think we'd move as a gathering

by yourself alone second movement of rosy transparency

make the move by yourself move out of this purple light

that ma—mah—moo-euve-veh time it's time to make a move

come let's waltz time did you think it'd be let's waltz

move as a gathering did you think we would move together

the second movement is the movement of rosy transparency

move out of this purple light move out of deep red light

to make a move ma—mah—moo-euve-veh it's time to move

it's time to move time for some passion in this language.

Doorway without a door

the doorway always open

almost the last doorway

one at a time inside

I am one the I me one

a sentence is a choice

I am the child of pain

the primitive I inside

inside the turbulence

almost the last time

inside the black rooms.

Away from the weddings wedding rooms

I have performed the first movement

I have made the movement of resignation

I have moved away all the way away

from those rooms into this black room

this is a different kind of domination

screaming within that will not decay

echoes of one scream within itself

seething and writhing within this room

away from the weddings wedding rooms

from those rooms into this black room

I am not making a move toward ladders

I am wandering again within this room.

I am wandering again within this room

I am not making a move toward ladders

from those rooms into this black room

away from the weddings wedding rooms

seething and writhing within this room

echoes of one scream within itself

screaming within that will not decay

this is a different kind of domination

from those rooms into this black room

I have moved away all the way away

I have made the movement of resignation

I have performed the first movement

away from the weddings wedding rooms.

Red deepened by black red made deep by black

unutterable depth of deep red brought out

what was unutterable brought out in one room

one picture in one room one room full of blood

room where the second movement is to be made

movement of rosy transparency the self rosy

self relating to self willing to be itself

the self itself in this room self transparent

rosy transparency through power of the blood

room where the second movement is to be made

where everything's given everything given back

where the guest enters and welcome is given

bride and groom take hands in warm welcome

the bride and groom take hands in their hands

I am in this room I do not make the movement

don't complete movement I'm the child of pain

I'm the child willing to be that child self

not burning Vietnamese child not Christ child

not rosy not transparent I'm the child of pain.

Doorway without a door

the doorway always open

the last without a door

one at a time outside

I am the one the I me one

I don't stop being one

I am the child of pain

the primitive I outside

inside the turbulence

there is no last time

inside the black rooms.

Tourists leave Chapel explosions of their talk

giggles of college girls "could you paint that?"

someone doubts Passion of Christ is the theme

someone dislikes hearing about "blood paintings"

I know a woman who was married in the Chapel

the paintings turned out black in her pictures

blue sky humid afternoon it's Spring in Houston

underneath peeling blue sky I see this red sky

there are swallows darting over a shallow pool

flower beside pool tiny florets like bow ties

ground where the flower grows turns deep red

this ground that keeps turning deep red ground.

Monk

1

A-bide   a-   a-

bide

               fast falls

             the   tide

             fast

the darkness deepens

2

        with   abide

        with

When others   fail

                    fail

                    fail

       comforts flee

        fail   flee

3

abide with me

abide with me

me   me

Marvin Gaye Suite

1

17 seconds of party formulaics by professional football players
intro of 17 seconds of hey man what's happening and right on
party of those gathered to be laid by the voice that lays
don't have to be a jock to be gathered brought together for the lay
Marvin mixed over the party Marvin calls out twice to mother
surely mother must be the answer forget about the father's tongue
if not one then the other not father unexpected relief of the other
mother blackens her breast mother goes to bed with father
Marvin left with the father Marvin calls three times to father
Marvin calls father father father we don't need to escalate
Marvin calls out three times to father within the father's house
isn't this ironic you probably can't help but feel superior
calling out three times to father in the house of the father's voice
listening to Marvin I want to cry it makes me want to cry
like Edgar witnessing the maddened king arraigning his daughters
isn't this ironic calling to father in the father's house
another call can he get a witness somebody somewhere
and in the mean time it's right on baby it's right on right on
I'm a witness I'll talk to him so I can see what's going on
what's going on party of those gathered brought together for the lay
party of those gathered to be laid by the voice that lays
those who believe that to linger and tarry is to be sheltered
I'll talk to Marvin I'll talk to you who have yet to be brought together
what's going on what's always going on in the house of the voice.

2

Bass figure fat half note two eighths another two and hold
"I'd attribute the Motown sound to Jamie Jamerson's busy bass"
sound there before Motown sound of the voice busy before the bass
Marvin wants to know what's happening the voice is what is
the busy voice is what's happening what is happening across this land
Marvin wants to know what else's new 'cause he's slightly behind
nothing else what is what's happening the voice is what's happening
Jamerson died of complications from a heart attack in Los Angeles
Marvin stopped "Sexual Healing" show to pray for his soul
Marvin stopped asking for that sexy rhythm for that sexy beat
"and the beat was largely the invention of Jamie Jamerson"
the voice busy before the bass the beat the voice's invention
to pray is to stop asking to pray is to be silent to remain silent
silent remain silent until the voice is heard the voice of the father
isn't this ironic you probably can't help but feel superior
isn't this ironic to stop asking for that rhythm for that beat
to stop asking be silent until sound of the father's voice is heard
the busy voice is what's happening what is happening across this land
would it do any good to pray for Marvin who doesn't understand
would it do any good to pray do any good to pray for Marvin's soul
I'm a witness wandering witness not praying I'm wandering
wandering means moving with the wrong rhythm on the wrong beat
listening to Marvin I want to cry it makes me want to cry
I'm a witness I'm wandering not praying wandering on the wrong beat.

3

It's not doo it's who Marvin taught how to fix his mouth muscles
it's who-who-who Marvin taught to make his breath part of the sound
his breath part of the phrasing his breath part of the sound
the sound there before Marvin the sound of the voice busy before Marvin
it's not who-who-who it's *oooooo—oooooo—oooooo* it's a hook
it's a hook made smooth made so very smooth *oooooo—oooooo—oooooo*
the singer has been hooked so very smooth that he hardly feels it
so smooth *oooooo—oooooo—oooooo* so smooth he hardly feels it
what the singer feels is elation and elegance and exultation
he's part of the sound part of the sound of the voice
what the singer feels is a high he's flying high in the friendly sky
Marvin thought cocaine was the boy who made slaves out of men
it's not cocaine it's the word and child who fixed Marvin's mouth
so smooth *oooooo—oooooo—oooooo* so smooth he hardly feels it
the singer feels he's flying rest of the folks lay their bodies down
party of those gathered to be laid by the voice that lays
hooked and gathered by the voice through Marvin's voice to be laid
those gathered feel their faces being eaten away they don't care
been hooked so very smooth the folks want to linger they want to tarry
hook made smooth made so very smooth *oooooo—oooooo—oooooo*
you can think you won't be hooked by the hook of the father's voice
you can think you won't be hooked by the hook of the singer's voice
Marvin thought cocaine was the boy who made slaves out of men
you can think you won't be hooked by the voice through Marvin's voice.

4

I just want to ask about world in despair world destined to die
what would that be would be without hope would be that world
without hope of kingdom to come without the river of water of life
river of water of life clear as crystal proceeding out of the throne
children held in the crystal river thread of remembrance severed
world without hope of kingdom to come that would be that world
that the river would dry up it would river dried-up riverbed
Marvin asks who really cares who's willing to try to save a world
he means world of hope of kingdom to come he means this river world
isn't this ironic asking to save this world that will not die
this world of hope of kingdom to come father's world that won't die
Marvin wants to save this world for the children let's save the children
let's save the children (spoken) let's save all the children (spoken)
save the babies (sung) quick fill on soprano save the babies (sung)
"perhaps the single most emotional moment he ever reached on record"
Marvin used multitracking to sing with himself speaking and singing
his singing voice higher than his speaking almost a woman's voice
speaking and singing the sound of the voice through his voice
I just want to ask a question what we're saving all the children for
what we're saving all the children for saving them to be laid
this is the father's world this world won't die father's voice won't
saving the children to be gathered together in this world of hope
children in river of water of life proceeding out of the throne
children in the crystal river the thread of remembrance severed.

5

Downshift from dig it everybody to think about it to talk about it

three times from Marvin don't go and talk about my father

the warning given three times don't go and talk about my father

three times the warning given in a voice made smooth so very smooth

don't want to don't want to and have to have to talk about father

I'll tell you I'm a witness I'll tell you what's going on

what's going on party of those gathered brought together for the lay

gathered by father's voice through Marvin's voice to be laid

one reason Marvin loved father was because he offered him Jesus

Marvin was thrilled and fascinated with the idea of tarrying

that's where you wait where you repeat over and over

over and over thank you Jesus repeat over and over thank you Jesus

where you repeat over and over thank you Jesus for minutes and hours

repetition is choice you choose to be part of the party that waits

those who believe that to linger and tarry is to be sheltered

Vaughan the Silurist warns of the deliberate search for idle words

of the leaving of *parricides* behind and no other monument

as if there needed to be another as if any other monument were needed

this is the father's world it won't die father's voice won't

don't want to don't want to and have to have to talk about father

Marvin was shot twice by his father on April 1, 1984 in Los Angeles

Marvin was shot twice by his father in his father's house

yes if you linger and tarry you will be sheltered in his house

in his house are many mansions in his house there are many parties.

6

Shared term between last song and this song the term is mercy
when you call on him for mercy father he'll be merciful my friend
Marvin knows when you call on him he'll be merciful
when you call there's response it's that old call and response
call and response of the father's voice sound of the father's voice
"sound unites groups of living beings as nothing else does"
united gathered by the sound of the father's voice through Marvin
groups parties of those gathered brought together for the lay
house full of people from which no one as of yet has gone out
people in the house of the father's voice father's voice won't die
where did all the blue skies go is a question they can answer
went into the house the blue skies went into the father's house
the blue skies went into the father's house mercy mercy me the ecology
people call for mercy and there's the sound of the father's voice
blue skies call and there's the smooth and zealous sound
call and response of the father's voice sound of the father's voice
sound unites groups of those who were living as nothing else
ah things are what they used to be ah what they used to and ever will be
same as they ever were give Mr. Byrne some credit same as they were
there has got to be a way Mr. Byrne's burning down the house
Pointer Sisters are burning they're burning doing the neutron dance
the house won't burn the father's house won't burn down to the ground
Marvin's in the house Marvin knows when you call on him for mercy
call and response of the father's voice sound of the father's voice.

7

Oh feel it feel it oh everybody feel it Marvin knows that's all right

he knows that's all right people oh when we're loved by the father

the father knows that's all right Marvin knows that's all right

everybody feel it at the love party of those gathered brought together

those gathered by the voice through Marvin's voice to be laid

sound of Marvin's voice good to party fun to party with you baby

sound of Marvin's voice the thrill is real and it's oh so good baby

Marvin pronounces "thrill" so that it rhymes with "real"

Marvin was thrilled and fascinated with the idea of tarrying

over and over thank you Jesus until you feel your face being eaten away

feel it feel it everybody the thrill is real and it's oh so good baby

Marvin feels there's only time for praying and for a love party

to pray is to stop asking is to be silent to remain silent

Marvin sings the lord's prayer on his *Dream of a Lifetime* album

the singer has been hooked so very smooth that he hardly feels it

those gathered feel the thrill of the father's tongue against their teeth

if you let him Marvin will take you to live where love is king

Marvin will take you where love is king the king and his secret life

love four times in a row love four times so smooth and so zealous

listening to Marvin I want to cry it makes me want to cry

like Edgar crying through his babble song *I smell the blood*

isn't this ironic you probably can't help but feel superior

there has got to be a way and there is no way out of the house

I'm a witness wandering not praying wandering in the house of the voice.

8

Holy to be wholly holy is to be wholly the excrement of the voice
the excrement the stinking fruit the stinking darkness in the low cars
to be wholly holy is to be in the low cars in the train of the voice
come together people got to get together to be wholly holy
you've got to believe whatever lingers and tarries is sheltered
there can be a train in the house there can be many trains in the house
you can pull the train at the love party of those gathered together
those gathered by the voice through Marvin's voice to be laid
sound of Marvin's voice good to party fun to party with you baby
you can pull the love train baby right on honey right on
you can pull the love train baby and you can repeat thank you Jesus
one reason Marvin loved his father was he offered him Jesus
Jesus left a long time ago said he would return kingdom to come
he left us a book to believe in we've got an awful lot to learn
Marvin says we'd better believe it Marvin says we've got a lot to learn
we've got to learn he is returned kingdom to come is kingdom come
this is the father's world this world won't die father's voice won't
we've got to learn it's too late to play dead in the low cars
Aretha sings "Wholy Holy" on her *Amazing Grace* album
Aretha makes up new words to go with Marvin's song as she goes along
moving and grooving with love doing and fooling with love
Southern California Community Choir behind her it's not doo it's who
it's not who it's *oooooo—ooo—ooo—oooooo* so smooth and so zealous
if it could only be that night silent night across the nation.

9

Heartbeat rhythm of the bass heartbeat rhythm across this land
Marvin said if we stop if we listen to the rhythm of our heartbeat
Marvin said we'll hear the rhythm of the father's voice
the sound there before Motown sound of the voice before the bass
if we stop long enough we'll be gathered brought together by the voice
if we stop long enough we'll be laid by the voice that lays
da-*duh* da-*duh* da-*duh* da-*duh* da-*duh* da-*duh* da-*duh* da-*duh* da-*duh*
that the heart would be torn out da-*duh* da-*duh* da-*duh*
heartbeat rhythm Marvin said his church lived within his own heart
would be torn out da-*duh* da-*duh* da-*duh* da-*duh* da-*duh* da-*duh* da-*duh*
the way they did his life it makes him want to holler
Marvin thought they were the lawyers the lawyers from the government
Marvin thought cocaine was the boy who made slaves out of men
it's the word and child who fixed Marvin's mouth it's the father
it's the father who fixed Marvin's mouth his father in his heart
in the Chicago Museum of Science and Industry there's a model heart
model heart to walk in children held by their parents
what the children hear is da-*duh* da-*duh* da-*duh* da-*duh* da-*duh*
listening to Marvin what I hear is da-*duh* da-*duh* da-*duh* da-*duh* da-*duh*
listening to Marvin I want to cry it makes me want to cry
listening to Marvin I want to holler and throw up both my hands
like Edgar under the weight of this sad time this same sad time
I'm a witness I'm wandering not praying in the house of the voice
I'm wandering not grooving wandering moving to the wrong beat.

Not Quite Parallel Lines

1

One end of the column in pencil larger than the other
out of the larger emerges still another column
actually two columns in pencil emerge from the first
the conjoined columns graphs of pitch against time
the first is held out held like an arm in blessing
the second column descends widens as it descends
end of the second is wide and the beginning of third
the third is a column of fire with hissing points

two lines two not quite parallel lines in extension
if the two lines were colored they would be colored red

sequence of the film follows sequence of the music
the poem is a sequence from graphs of pitch against time
in the film I'm arrested for not letting the child be born
sequence I can look out the kitchen windows of my house
the judgement of judge and jury judgement of guilty
sequence I cannot look out and I cannot walk up and down
they'll walk with me they will walk hand in hand with me
diagnosis of the doctor is a kind of sickness of silence
sequence in isolation in my own house with all its stairs
always it seems I'm always on the route to releasement.

2

Sound backwards sound can be made to pass backwards
made to pass backwards to its source by graphs
begin with extinction of sound and end with the attack
the attack is a diamond shape that becomes an arrow

by definition the arrow belongs to the class of weapons
fragments have been found throughout the country
the fragments mean that it has always been with us
has always been with us the arrow that flieth by day

it can enter the air with a minimum of resistance
edge opened only a slit then a resounding tearing

the searching for an edge and then the tearing
this is the constant humdrum constant humdrum of life

a present with its point intact and gift-wrapped
Sam & Dave: "wrap it up / I'll take it" always taking it
impossible in fact to carry on business without it
but something no one in his right mind would dwell on.

3

The waves spread out and out from one source of power
the question is where will you and I position ourselves
there is the source of power and there is the wave
the waves spread out to become one standing wave
one standing wave from one source which is the horn
the one wave which is a kind of arrow a kind of weapon

to look directly down into the mouth of the horn
who would not think twice about calling it "my" horn
into the power supply the oscillator the resonator
like peeping to secrets through a strange bird's eyes
this is where the growl and the shout come from
the horn is the instrument of the growl and the shout
who would have dreamed the horn must be opposed
I must oppose the horn by deformation of association

back to the wave and to the question of position
the wave may become a blade broad as the horizon itself
or it may become narrow with a sharp point wrapped in fire
whether horizon or wrapped point the question remains

agreed oh what a beautiful morning is one position
the moon faint crescent still out and high up in the sky.

These tongues of fire from the mouth of the horn
who knows what tongues sound like sound like hissing
pity for those who lie out on the tongues
mercy pity peace and love consumed by the tongues of fire

the flexed arm has little need of a hammer
there is more than sufficient power in the arm
arm that is that arm that is arm and horn of power
arm and horn not held like an arm in blessing after all

two lines again two not quite parallel lines again
they are like the opened mouth seen from the side
an abstraction or schematic of the opened mouth
it also could be said to be on its way to possibility

dump truck from Selmer delivers its load of glow
its load pours out in not quite parallel lines
faithful from the One Mind Temple position themselves
the faithful position themselves "to feel the glow"

repeated cries of warning from those who lie out
what are their cries in comparison with the tongues
what can their cries do against the class of weapons
their shrill cries can do nothing against glowing weapons

the red tongues fully extended from the opened mouth
body of the tongues and tip of the tongues extended
the tongues neither Dionysius' nor a dinosaur's
tongues of the typhonian voice letting them all hang out.

5

Uncovered Vine's seen by the rifled sepulcher of kings
he is one of the funeral men who puzzle and tease
one who would withhold the key even from friends
it may be the cross-purposes of life make one shy
make for a quiet man who won't be touched by argument
how know such a man "except in shadow from the wing"

heir to funeral man throwing stones at his shadow
the one who is throwing stones at his own shadow
and to the other one neither one a euphonist of academe
the other one who speaks to fill trying pauses
the one whose supplement is life in boats and tents
one the other I am heir to these exceptional natures

and to two other funeral men who are two black men
two black men who are "blues people" two horn players
one experienced an awakening during the year 1957
was revealed to one he had the right seal in his forehead

the horn is the instrument of the growl and the shout
and if and if the horn what of the scratching pen
who would have dreamed that there must be opposition
heir to and opponent of these exceptional natures.

Bell of the horn the bell or mouth directly overhead
naked men upside-down naked men play overhead
world in flames typifies the end and the beginning
skeleton heads smiling into the mouth of the horn

the hand strikes against the hand at obtuse angles
glancing blows hand against hand like cymbals
hands entranced in the gaps in between the beats
hand against hand bleeding hands bone against bone

I looked at the lily at bones as leaves and petals
ring of the flower ring of the flower's thought
now the motion is different turned into slow motion
ring now excrement of the voice slow train of excrement

perhaps nothing more than the stereotypical chase scene
special effects adult language some violence
see this horn drives people crazy then it eats their
call a spade a spade then it eats their faces away

two lines again two not quite parallel lines again
lines of the opened mouth the class of weapons
wavy lines wavy glowing lines pulling the disco crowd in
the glowing lines from an old tune "Blessed Assurance."

The player is breathed through completely and gently

through so completely so gently he hardly feels it

the player of the horn which drives people crazy

the player feels elation and elegance and exaltation

people put hands in put their whole selves in the gaps

what the people feel is their faces being eaten away

the player experienced an awakening during the year 1957

the player is not a perturbation of the voice's breath

I've been arrested for not letting the child be born

been arrested for not letting the child be born in me

for not letting the word and child be born in me

word and child another kind of instrument of the voice

two lines again two not quite parallel lines again

of the opened mouth the class of weapons word and child

paint and ink on vellum a page from the Apocalypse

the horn is sounded followed by hissing hail and fire

hissing hail and fire mingled with blood on the earth

the player's erect not a fold of his garments disturbed.

The horn sounded summons sounded and a raggedy march
summons and a march and suddenly crying and whimpering
growl from the back of the throat rough R&B growl
shout from the back of the throat rough R&B shout
the growl and the shout recorded live June 14, 1964
and whimpering bloody heads running out in the night

it was revealed to him that he had the right seal
the player is not a perturbation of the voice's breath

use a stack of amps use another another and another
turn them up turn them up to get a wall of sound
turn them all up until your ears are washed in blood
turn them up and still not close to the voice's breath

the player thought your strength was in your blood
bloody head blood down your face not close to the voice

paint and ink on vellum a page from the Apocalypse
the horn is sounded burning mountain cast into the sea
hissing as the burning mountain is cast into the sea
the player's erect not a fold of his garments disturbed.

9

Come down to one word who would've dreamed one word

this one terrible word even this doesn't mean the end

there can be opposition by deformation of one word

there can be opposition to the humming of one word

I like to write something that people can't hum

that people can't hum can't put entranced hands in

people can't put entranced hands together in the gaps

can't put their whole entranced selves in the gaps

one end of the column is larger than the other

the end of the second is wide and beginning of third

I am twisting these conjoined columns of the horn

deforming the horn trying to deform the horn of the voice.

Poem Beginning with a Line by Traherne

A tree apprehended is a tree in your mind

black locust with its bark put on in slabs

seams between the slabs ivy around them

the ivy around the trunk and further up

branches of the tree all their divarication

branches of the tree out over lawn and garden

myriad tiny leaves myriad tiny reflectors

leaves reflect leaves in parallel rows

the several parts of the tree extended in space

bark trunk branches tiny leaves extended

this extension is in your mind's apprehension

your mind's full with the parts of the tree

your mind is full and the air is pocked

the air this morning is pocked with emptiness.

Reflexive

Consider whether you can be solitary and alone

whether you can sit alone like a sparrow

like a sparrow in an indentation in the ground

an indentation in the deep red ground

consider whether you can be like this in a valley

valley of vision where the ground is deep red

valley of vision where there are no roses

where there is not even a secret rose

consider whether you can remain in such a valley

in a valley of vision which is always the same

where the ground is always deep red ground

where there is not even a secret rose

consider whether you can remain like a sparrow

whether you can sit alone like a sparrow

like a sparrow in an indentation in the ground

in a valley of vision which is always the same.

At Arrowhead

Whether seeing after seeing is of any use

whether after-seeing can preserve shadows

the shadows of ferns their ambiguity

whether there can be shadows without invasion.

Whether this kind of seeing is of any use

whether the shadows can be preserved

shadows of what was howling wilderness

whether there can be shadows without invasion.

Whether long sought after seeing is of use

whether shadows should be preserved

shadows of mountains playing hide-and-seek

whether there can be shadows without invasion.

Whether this seeing was ever of any use

whether there should be preservation

shadows of clouds blackening the mountains

whether there can be shadows without invasion.

FROM

Crosses: Poems 1992–1998
2005

A Number of Times

The son steps into what he heard was empty
the son steps into the empty house of his father
the son steps into what he had heard was empty
the son steps into and is seized and bitten
the son steps into and is bitten a number of times
the son steps into only to be seized and bitten
the son steps into what he's heard was empty
the son steps into the house of his father
the son steps into what he heard was to be empty.

Before that step there could be other steps

there could be other steps before that

there could be many and other steps

there could be so many steps before that step.

2

The son steps into what he heard was empty
the son steps into the empty house of his father

the son steps into and is seized and bitten
the son steps into and is bitten a number of times

the son steps into what he's heard was empty
the son steps into the house of his father

Before that step there could be other steps
it's always possible to imagine other steps
there could be other steps before that

there could be many and other steps
always possible to imagine many and other steps
there could be so many steps before that step.

3

the son steps into the empty house of his father

the son steps into and is bitten a number of times

the son steps into the house of his father

Before that step there could be other steps
it's always possible to imagine other steps
there could be other steps before that
ever felt a gentle touch then a kiss
there could be many and other steps
always possible to imagine many and other steps
there could be so many steps before that step.

Sainte-Chapelle

in memory of Olivier Messiaen

Specifically the rose window specifically the center

center of the rose left to right bottom to top

left to right the receiver kneeling with tightly closed eyes

kneeling before orange claws of the sender

candlestick elaborate nail there are several nails

hand of the sender reaches toward a nail

sitting in black and purple robes sitting on a rainbow

sender on green rainbow reaching toward a nail

four stars pale yellow stars eruptions out of the blue

eruptions out of the blue that will not heal

sender wears a knot of deeper yellow

receiver prays to untie the knot prays and suffers

on each side of the sender a nail ever-ready nail

between the nails a two-edged sword

sender holds a two-edged sword in his mouth

sword in his mouth his mouth a black X stretching wide.

Precious Lord

Not sweet sixteen not even sweet sixteen and she's moaning

not even sixteen years old and she's moaning

not even sweet sixteen and she's moaning the words

moaning out the words to "Precious Lord"

she says "ain't no harm to moan" and she's moaning

it's Aretha in the New Bethel Baptist Church in Detroit in 1956

words moaned out so that she becomes denuded

no more little black dress she has nothing to hide

no more little black dress she has nothing left to hide.

Thomas Dorsey wrote the words wrote the words and the music

Thomas Dorsey wrote the words and the music for "Precious Lord"

Thomas Dorsey aka Georgia Tom wrote other songs

one of the other songs "Deep Moaning Blues"

Thomas Dorsey: "I like the long moaning groaning tone"

Georgia Tom moaned "Deep Moaning Blues" with Ma Rainey

Georgia Tom and Ma Rainey moan they moan and groan

their moaning and groaning make you see

moaning and groaning you're made to see they have nothing.

2

The first time Mahalia does it as one interconnected phrase

she does it as three in one three words in one phrase

three in one: "take-en-n—my-ah-aah—ha-an-nd"

Mahalia does it in the same year in 1956 the same year as Aretha

same but different the second time it is more aggressive

it's more aggressive: "take-ake my-ah han-and"

Mahalia was a big fine woman Mahalia was denuded

she sang "Precious Lord" at the funeral of Martin Luther King

Aretha sang "Precious Lord" at the funeral of Mahalia.

Thomas Dorsey met Mahalia met her for the first time in 1928

it was in 1928 that Georgia Tom moaned with Ma Rainey

he moaned with Ma Rainey he moaned and he groaned with Ma Rainey

he met Mahalia and he taught her how to moan

"you teach them how to say their words in a moanful way"

to say their words how to say his words

Mahalia was a big fine woman Mahalia was denuded

Dorsey knew the heavier the voice the better the singer

Dorsey knew as any teacher knows the heavier the better.

3

Al Green has a softened voice he has a voice made softened

he was made to sing softened by Willie Mitchell in 1972

softened and softened and softened

Al Green became Rev. Al Green of the Full Gospel Tabernacle in 1980

a tabernacle is a fixed or movable habitation

habitation where you stay together with the lord

Al Green has a softened voice he has a voice made softened

he was made to sing softened on "Let's Stay Together"

in 1982 he was made to sing softened on "Precious Lord."

Photograph of Thomas Dorsey photograph of a smooth operator

photograph of Georgia Tom photo of a smooth operator

the photo smoothed out retouched softened

one side of the face completely light one side of the face all dark

one side merges into the light smoothed out softened

one side merges into the dark smoothed out made softened

in the photograph a smooth operator is lighting a cigarette

slender fingers hold a matchbox hold a match

slender fingers hold a softened flame against the softened dark.

4

"Lead me" sing "lead me" they move with a repetitive rhythm

Dom Mocquereau: "rhythm is the ordering of the movement"

repetitive rhythm orders them to move on "lead"

they move with all their weight on "lead" it sounds like "feed"

it's the Soul Stirrers it's the most rhythmic music you ever heard

repetitive rhythm it sounds like "*feed* me"

S.R. Crain tenor A.L. Johnson baritone J.J. Farley bass

Edmond Jabès: "can we be healed by repetition?"

the Soul Stirrers move with a repetitive rhythm sing "*feed* me."

Thomas Dorsey came to Chicago came looking for deliverance

Georgia Tom came in 1916 the Soul Stirrers in 1937

to get deliverance you have to wait on the movements of providence

he played piano he sang at buffet flats at rent parties

he was a smooth player and he sang softly

a smooth player they called him "the whispering piano player"

the most popular dance at the parties was the slow drag

he learned how to drag easy how to sing softly

how to drag easy how to wait on the movements of providence.

Soul Stirrers move with a repetitive rhythm sing "*feed* me"

repetitive rhythm orders them to sing "*feed* me"

R.H. Harris sings lead he sings the essential word

R.H. Harris taught Sam Cooke and Sam Cooke taught Johnny Taylor

Johnny Taylor "Who's Making Love" 1968

R.H. Harris: "they got a touch of me even if they don't know me"

what they got a touch of touch of tongue love

R.H. Harris taught them to study the essential word

the word brings it to a picture it's the lord making love.

Thomas Dorsey wrote the words wrote the words and the music

Thomas Dorsey wrote the words wrote the essential word

wrote "precious" not "blessed" the essential word is "precious"

this was to be enshrined as a moment of epiphany

moment when he wrote the better-sounding word

moment of *épiphanie epiphania epiphano epiphaneia epiphanies*

moment of epiphany essential word shining picture

Dorsey: "that thing like something hit me and went all over me"

that thing must be that same thing went all over him.

6

Clara Ward's real nasal her nasality makes her a real moaner

she moans the three in one three words in one word

she moans so that one word becomes three

one becomes three: "thru-uuu-uah"

double-clutches just like Aretha: "thru-ah thru-uuu-uah the night"

sounds just like Aretha because Aretha sounds just like her

Aretha followed Clara Ward note for moaning note

denuded Aretha followed denuded Clara

and did Aretha follow her to the lord to the lord to the light.

Thomas Dorsey was invited to Philadelphia by Gertrude Ward

Mrs. Gertrude Mae Murphy Ward the mother of Clara

in 1931 Mrs. Ward was told in a vision was told to go and to sing

Dorsey was invited to teach the Wards how to sing

how to say his words in a moanful way

Dorsey liked the long moaning groaning tone

Mrs. Ward was told in a vision a vision from the lord

Dorsey taught Clara and Clara taught Aretha

how to say his words in a moanful way all through the night.

7

Sounds like "*feed* me" doesn't sound like the Soul Stirrers

it's not the Soul Stirrers it's the Kings of Harmony

the Kings of Harmony with Carey Bradley on lead

Carey Bradley was taught by Silas Steele the first hard lead

Silas Steele sang lead for the Blue Jay Singers

those singers recorded the first quartet version of a Dorsey song

Silas Steele sang hard with a repetitive rhythm

question is can we be healed by repetition

over "feed me" Carey Bradley sings hard: "take-ah my hand."

Blue Jay Singers the first quartet to record a Dorsey song

in 1931 those singers recorded "If You See My Saviour"

those singers: "if you see my saviour tell him that you saw me"

in 1931 Georgia Tom recorded "Please Mr. Blues"

Georgia Tom recorded in 1931 with Tampa Red

Georgia Tom and Tampa Red recorded a low moaning blues

"Please Mr. Blues" is a deep low-down moaning blues

those singers: "please be careful handle me like a child"

if you saw their saviour you would see Mr. Blues.

8

Brother Joe May has a big voice has a big and loud voice

Brother Joe May the thunderbolt of the Middle West

the way he sang "pra-aaa-aaa-aaa-shus" is like thunder

he was taught to sing "pra-aaa-aaa-aaa-shus" by Mother Smith

he was taught to sing by Mother Willie Mae Ford Smith

she was called Mother he called her Mother

Mother Smith: "the lord just anoints me while I'm singing"

when you're anointed something goes all over you

must be that same thing went all over her went all over her son.

Mrs. Willie May introduced "If You See My Saviour" in 1930

this was before she was called Mother

twenty years before Brother Joe May sang "pra-aaa-aaa-aaa-shus"

in 1930 in Chicago at the National Baptist Convention

during the morning devotions at the convention

she sang "you saw me" during the morning devotions

in 1930 in Chicago Georgia Tom recorded "She Can Love So Good"

in 1931 in Chicago Georgia Tom recorded "Please Mr. Blues"

if you saw her you'd see Mr. Blues loving her so good.

Way past sixteen way past sweet sixteen and she's moaning

she says "when I don't feel like singing I moan"

it's Sister Rosetta Tharpe at The Hot Club de France in 1966

Sister Rosetta had dyed her hair red played a hollow-body jazz guitar

Sister Rosetta has a resonating vibrato

she moans "ho-oo-oo-oo-meh" with a resonating vibrato

she moans out "ho-oo-oo-oo-meh" becomes resonant

"when I don't feel like singing I moan"

she becomes completely resonant she has nothing left to hide.

Thomas Dorsey wrote the words wrote the words and the music

Thomas Dorsey wrote the words and the music for "Precious Lord"

the song is an answer song to another song

answer to George Nelson Allen's "Must Jesus Bear the Cross Alone?"

George Nelson Allen thought the answer was no

a cross for everyone "there's a cross for everyone"

Thomas Dorsey thought the answer was no

"see you got to be susceptible for whatever comes in the ear"

he got Sister Rosetta to be susceptible got everyone susceptible.

In Croce

How many faces how many faces can you count in the tree

children's counting game one of the games of the child mind

counting game of my own child of pain mind

how many eaten away faces can you count on the cross

one of the faces I count on the cross blind and black face

blind and black man's face without his shades

blind and black man's face without his three horns

blind and black man's without his shades and his three horns

one of the tunes he once played: "Old Rugged Cross"

whole lot of things been bothering blind and black man

he said he was here to tell all y'all

here to tell all y'all that we got a cross that we must bear

blind and black man thought he could deal with it

thought he could deal with it he thought he could leave it alone

what he didn't think that it wouldn't leave him alone

didn't think his blind and black face would be on the cross.

2

One of the faces I count on the cross face of the green man

green face of the green man among leaves

green man disappeared among leaves and fruit

almost completely disappeared among stinking fruit

green face of the green man was not wasn't always green

wasn't green before he was nailed to the cross

the man imagined the cross to be a tree with leaves and fruit

curing every sickness having every delight

Betty Carter will tell you: imagination is funny

it can make a cross a tree with leaves and fruit

leaves and fruit having every delight sweetness of every taste

imagination can make a cross with the taste of a bride

the green man thought he could linger with her

could linger with her like a bundle of myrrh between her breasts

green face of green man nailed to the cross

face of the man almost disappeared among stinking fruit.

3

One of the faces I count I count the face of a white woman

face of a white woman in pain white woman's pain face

her face in pain because of a seed inside her

seed of "most beautiful tree" seed of the cross inside her

she wouldn't have opened her door if she had known

she wouldn't have said you better come on in to my kitchen

she wouldn't have opened her door

she wouldn't have said come she wouldn't have said yes

pale white forehead darkly lustrous hair parted pale white forehead

curved ever so slightly curved eyebrows

slightly curved slightly curved slightly thinned

eyes under the eyebrows as round as darkly lustrous as cherries

her pale white forehead contracted in pain

ever so slightly curved eyebrows contracted in pain

curved slightly thinned eyebrows contracted in pain

cherry eyes under the eyebrows hollowed out and eaten away.

4

One of the faces I count I count the face of a white woman

face of a white woman in pain white woman's pain face

her face in pain because of a tree inside her

because of "most beautiful tree" because of the cross inside her

she opened her door she said better come on in to my kitchen

she said come on in she said yes

face of a white woman in pain white woman's pain face

she's in pain because of a tree inside her

a not imagined woman said only a betrayal could uproot it

tree could be uprooted if there could be a double-crossing woman

sock it to me backup group whispers to a white woman

sock it to me backup group whispers: tell it

only a double-crossing woman could

only she could tell the father's love like it is

face of a white woman in pain her face contracted in pain

she's trying to tell it she's trying to uproot a tree inside her.

5

Faces I count I count two faces the faces of two black men

blind and black face of the man who thought he could deal with it

black face of the man who said this is my story

faces of two black men on the cross criss-crossed faces

blind and black man thought he could deal with it

thought he could thought he could leave it

other black man said this is my story this is my song

said perfect submission perfect delight

other black man is a witness a witness is always blinded

witnesses of the father's love are always blinded

"witnessing substitutes narrative for perception"

my story my song because eyes have been hollowed out

this is my story this is my song

narrative of other man without eyes without shades without a piano

other black man said this is my story of submission

perfect submission perfect delight he said all is at rest.

6

One of the faces I count on the cross face of tempted man

tempted man tempted by the last temptation

imagine that there could be the last temptation

tempted by the temptation that there could be the last temptation

in the movie tempted man asks who's getting married

he asks and guardian angel tells him: you are

he's getting married he's not getting married in the morning

he's getting married to the bride who couldn't say no

the bride is wearing a long-sleeved white gown

very simple even severe gown more a shift than a gown

the bride is wearing a garland around her hair

very simple even severe garland of green leaves around her hair

the bride is not the last temptation

the last temptation is the ordinary life lure of that life

the bride will be taken away to die (not in the movie)

the life will be everything will be taken away from tempted man.

7

One of the faces not to be counted face of the lost one

the lost one the one who stays lost

imagine being lost imagine being the lost one

imagination's funny hard to imagine being the one who stays lost

"it's always a matter of returning from wandering"

blind and black man wouldn't say that green man wouldn't

white woman double-crossing woman wouldn't

other black man tempted man wouldn't

faces I count on the cross were the life of the party

their faces were the life of the father's party

faces returned to the father's love party returned and stayed

they returned they returned and they stayed

not able to stay lost not able to be lost and to stay lost

not able to imagine being lost staying lost

unable to imagine being the lost one who stays lost

take a good look: they returned they returned and they stayed.

Standing Wave

1993

Three Words from Thomas Bernhard

Of or for of the of the hearing of the hearing of hearing of the ear

or for or for the or for the hearing or for the hearing of

for the hearing of the ear the hearing of the ear is the object

I have written that you have to hear you have to you have to hear

have written that you have to give you have to you have to give ear

written that you who have ears to hear that you have to give ear

for the hearing of the ear the hearing of the ear is the object

or for or for the or for the hearing or for the hearing of

of or for of the of the hearing of the hearing of hearing of the ear

rumbling on the ground a rumbling within itself on the ground

the hearing of the ear is the object for the hearing of the ear

or for the hearing of or for the hearing or for the or for

hearing of the ear of the hearing of the hearing of of or for

you have to hear you have to I have written that you have to hear

you have to give ear you have to have written that you have to give

that you have to give ear written that you who have ears to hear

hearing of the ear of the hearing of the hearing of of or for

or for the hearing of or for the hearing or for the or for

the hearing of the ear is the object for the hearing of the ear.

The night was dark and without the father dark night and no father
no father was there dark night and without the father no father
no father was there dark night in which the little boy cried
the night was dark and without and the little boy began to cry
the little boy cried speak cried speak father to your little boy
the little boy cried speak father to your little boy or else
the little boy cried there was a rumbling there was a sudden flash
rumbling a rumbling within itself like the roar of an animal
roar of an animal with a golden mane flash of the animal's mane
roar of an animal kiss of an animal with its rough tongue
the animal kisses and wounds the little boy with its rough tongue.

The little boy tries to become smaller smallest in size or degree

tries to become very small tries to make his ear very small

within his smallness the little boy tries to make his ear very small

within his smallness the ear which hears the ear smallest of all

smallest of all within his smallness the ear cannot be a conduit

the little boy believes that this statement is certainly valid

the little boy tries to become smaller smallest in size or degree

he tries to become very small he tries to make his ear very small.

All the Steps

1

Those who hear the train they had better worry worry

those who hear they had better worry worry.

2

No disgrace to worry to have the worried life blues

might do some good to be worried in the hour of our need.

3

Run run run away going to run run run away

there are those who think they're going to run away.

4

To hear and to be facing and to be facing what is heard

to hear and to be face to face with what is heard.

5

Run run run away they're going to run run run away

there are those who think they're going to run away from the train.

6

Fort built to protect the community from desert raiders
community thought to protect itself from raiders.

7

Those who hear the train they had better worry worry
better worry worry about a gift of tears.

8

Those who are gathered in the fort had better learn
they had better learn how to cure their wounds.

9

The train with its poison and its tongue
the lurking train with its poison and its tongue.

10

Those who are gathered better learn to be insensitive
learn how to put on a show of being insensitive.

11

Danger of its poison and of its tongue

danger of its poison and of its tongue against our teeth.

12

Had better break the habit the habit of prayer

better let the jokes come back to us when we're at prayer.

13

What really kills me is standing in the need of prayer

standing in a gathering in the need of prayer.

14

Don't if we don't if we don't break the habit

we will be made to climb all the steps of the ladder.

15

Brood over someone else's dream: three-story red tower

beneath the tower the train is always departing.

16

Danger of its tongue for those gathered like a group

gathered like a group of all virgins with their downcast eyes.

17

There is this problem with cutting off the prayer hand

there is this problem with the other hand.

18

How insensitive is how those who hear better be

how insensitive how unmoved and cold they had better be.

19

You can call him you can call him up and ask him

if we had only asked for "Sleep Walk" by Santo & Johnny.

20

Red tower green sky three-story tower against green sky

beneath the tower the train is always departing.

21

Don't break it be made to climb all the steps

we don't break it we'll be made to climb all the steps.

22

Ant on the floor the small ant on the kitchen floor

the small ant anticipates by sound or shadow.

23

Light turns out in the kitchen when somebody pulls on the string

those gathered not able to anticipate the danger.

24

If we had only stayed in the school of the prophets

in the school of the prophets who catch thoughts from words.

25

Ant on the floor the small ant on the kitchen floor

those gathered not able to anticipate the danger.

26

Those who are gathered are fondled and taken by the hand
taken by the hand and made to climb all the steps.

27

Perfectly built fort bound to make the community unhappy
bound to make those in the community unhappy.

28

What really kills me is standing in the need of prayer
I'm standing in the need of jokes that come back.

29

Standing in the need of prayer in a perfectly built fort
bound to make you unhappy bound to make me unhappy.

30

Not broken the habit of prayer not been broken
those who are gathered better learn how to cure their wounds.

Standing Wave

1

Line to line connection of line to line with line to line
one line to line with one line to line at a time
connection of one line to line with one line to line
I connect one line to line with one line to line
connection of one line to line with one line to line at a time
within one line to line a room within one line to line
connection of one line to line with one line to line
one line to line with one line to line at a time
line to line connection of line to line with line to line
there is a standing wave so high in the middle of my room
the folds of the wave in perfect obedience
standing wave so high in the middle of my room
folds upon folds of the wave in perfect obedience
there is a standing wave so high I can't get over it
line to line connection of line to line with line to line
one line to line with one line to line at a time
connection of one line to line with one line to line
within one line to line a room within one line to line
connection of one line to line with one line to line at a time
I connect one line to line with one line to line
connection of one line to line with one line to line
one line to line with one line to line at a time
line to line connection of line to line with line to line.

2

Line to line with line to line connection of line to line

one line to line at a time with one line to line

line to line with one line to line connection of one

line to line with one line to line I connect one

line to line with one line to line at a time connection of one

within one line to line a room within one line to line

line to line with one line to line connection of one

one line to line at a time with one line to line

line to line with line to line connection of line to line

there is a standing wave soo-oo-o-oo high in the middle

foo-oo-o-oolds of wave in perfect obedience

standing wave soo-oo-o-oo high in the middle of my room

foo-oo-o-oolds upon foo-oo-o-oolds of the wave

standing wave soo-oo-o-oo high I can't get over it

line to line with line to line connection of line to line

one line to line at a time with one line to line

line to line with one line to line connection of one

within one line to line a room within one line to line

line to line with one line to line at a time connection of one

line to line with one line to line I connect one

line to line with one line to line connection of one

one line to line at a time with line to line

line to line with line to line connection of line to line.

3

Line to line disconnection of one line from line to line

line to line disconnection of one line to line

disconnection of one line to line from line to line

one line to line from two of the other line to line

one from two of the other to make an opening

I disconnect one line to line to make an opening in my room

disconnection of one line to line from line to line

line to line disconnection of one line to line

line to line disconnection of one line from line to line

there was a standing wave so wide in the middle of my room

the folds of the wave in perfect obedience

standing wave so wide in the middle of my room

folds upon folds of the wave in perfect obedience

there was a standing wave so wide I couldn't get around it

line to line disconnection of one line from line to line

line to line disconnection of one line to line

disconnection of one line to line from line to line

I disconnect one line to line to make an opening in my room

one from two of the other to make an opening

one line to line from two of the other line to line

disconnection of one line to line from line to line

line to line disconnection of one line to line

line to line disconnection of one line from line to line.

4

One line from line to line disconnection of line to line

one line to line disconnection of line to line

line to line from line to line disconnection of one

the other line to line one line to line from two

to make an opening one from two of the other

to make an opening in my room I disconnect one line to line

line to line from line to line disconnection of one

one line to line disconnection of line to line

one line from line to line disconnection of line to line

there was a standing wave soo-oo-o-oo wide in the middle

foo-oo-o-oolds of the wave in perfect obedience

standing wave soo-oo-o-oo wide in the middle of my room

foo-oo-o-oolds upon foo-oo-o-oolds of the wave

standing wave soo-oo-o-oo wide I couldn't get around it

one line from line to line disconnection of line to line

one line to line disconnection of line to line

line to line from line to line disconnection of one

to make an opening in my room I disconnect one line to line

to make an opening one from two of the other

the other line to line one line to line from two

line to line from line to line disconnection of one

one line to line disconnection of line to line

one line from line to line disconnection of line to line.

5

Line to line demarcation of line to line from line to line

demarcation of three line to line from line to line

three from line to line from other line to line

demarcation from other line to line by being made darker

three line to line demarcation of three by being made darker

I make three darker to make an opening in my room

three from line to line from other line to line

demarcation of three line to line from line to line

line to line demarcation of line to line from line to line

there will be a standing wave so deep in the middle of my room

the folds of the wave in perfect obedience

standing wave so deep in the middle of my room

folds upon folds of the wave in perfect obedience

there will be a standing wave so deep I won't get under it

line to line demarcation of line to line from line to line

demarcation of three line to line from line to line

three from line to line from other line to line

I make three darker to make an opening in my room

three line to line demarcation of three by being made darker

demarcation from other line to line by being made darker

three from line to line from other line to line

demarcation of three line to line from line to line

line to line demarcation of line to line from line to line.

6

Line to line from line to line demarcation of line to line

line to line from line to line demarcation of three

line to line from other line to line from three

being made darker demarcation from other line to line

demarcation of three by being made darker three line to line

to make an opening in my room I make three darker

line to line from other line to line from three

line to line from line to line demarcation of three

line to line from line to line demarcation of line to line

there will be a standing wave soo-oo-o-oo deep in the middle

foo-oo-o-oolds of the wave in perfect obedience

standing wave soo-oo-o-oo deep in the middle of my room

foo-oo-o-oolds upon foo-oo-o-oolds of the wave

there'll be a standing wave soo-oo-o-oo deep I won't get under it

line to line from line to line demarcation of line to line

line to line from line to line demarcation of three

line to line from other line to line from three

to make an opening in my room I make three darker

demarcation of three by being made darker three line to line

being made darker demarcation from other line to line

line to line from other line to line from three

line to line from line to line demarcation of three

line to line from line to line demarcation of line to line.

Pastorelles

2004

Thales the Milesian/In a Time of Drought

Thales the Milesian
the first philosopher of the first philosophers
philosophers or phusikoi
Thales the Milesian said that the earth floats on water
in some way the source of all

first of the first philosophers of material substance
the source of all existing things
that from which a thing first comes into being
and into which it is finally destroyed
the substance persisting

this is the element and first principle
and so there's no absolute coming to be or passing away
the substance persisting
the substance the source of all
and the first philosopher said it is water

other and later philosophers came up with the reasons
the seeds of all things are moist
warmth itself comes to be and lives by the moist
water is the principle of all moist things
corpses dry up.

In a time of drought

the time in the morning in a time

dry

already too dry and too warm

and without rain

all day the time remaining too dry and too warm

all day

day after day

in a time remaining too dry and too warm

too dry and too warm

and without rain

copper beeches

young leaves of the young copper beeches

shriveled-up shapes

corpses

these shriveled-up shapes in the shapes of corpses

shapes in the shapes of clutching.

William Bronk

Along the canal on a summer evening

where you recited your poem the poem about

the red at Sherman's farm

about red as a transformer on the dull barn and sheds

almost embarrassing

almost theatric

Shakespearean almost in the intonation of a moody Shakespearean king

recited to an audience of one

and you wanted to know if I knew the poem

and I did what I didn't know how red would transform me how

deeply

red after black would ingrain me.

Henry David Thoreau/Sonny Rollins

1

Two years and two months

alone in the woods

where he had vast range and circuit

his nights black kernels

never profaned by any human neighborhood

Rishyashringa

and no courtesan with a wound to be rubbed and to be kissed

who heard sounds in his nights

and no courtesan who heard the sounds of owls

sounding like

like *that I had never been born*

like *that I had never been born.*

2

Who rejoiced that there are owls

who rejoiced in reading

in reading the classics "the noblest recorded thoughts"

having spent youthful days

costly hours

learning words of an ancient language

an ancient language of perpetual suggestion and provocation

me phunai nikai

three little suggestions

perpetual

singing if it can be called singing

to sing along with the sounds of owls.

3

Cut of the slash

which cuts

which cuts and which connects

mark

of the cut of

time itself

which leaves a blue mark

black and blue mark

which can be read as a kind of bridge

connecting black and blue and

the abstract truth of

time itself.

4

Fled the clubs

nightclubs meccas of smoke clatter

and chatter amid smoke murmur and murmur of assignation

hegira

for two years

alone with the alone

alone with the alone saxophone

in the air

alone in the night air and high above the East River

heimarmene and black water of the river

without a you to do a something to a me

without a song in the air.

5

In the night air

the seven planets in material orbits

so huge and moving at so great a speed must produce sound

harmonia of heimarmene

ringing and roaring sound the sound of a grinding down

"heavenly harmony" in waves and particles

in the air in the ear in the heart

since birth

in the heart there is a melody of heaven's harmony

ringing and roaring

alone with that

without a song with that.

Magdalene Poem

Love enters the body

enters

almost

almost completely breaks and enters into the body

already beaten and broken

peaceful if breaking if breaking

and entering the already broken is peaceful

untouchable fortunately

untouchable.

In the Kitchen

1

Someone someone's in the kitchen

old lady someone's old finger

a design a sign old lady someone's leathery old finger that points

someone's in the kitchen with a brown-haired girl

who is wearing a gold-brown tunic over a grey-brown skirt

brown-eyed girl

brown-haired and brown-eyed

fingers of the girl in a fist around a pestle

silver mortar reflecting brown table

on the brown table broken garlic clove dried red pepper

plate of four silvery grey-brown fish four fish with four fish eyes

brown and shiny black pitcher

beside plate and pitcher

black skillet

in the skillet a silver spoon two unbroken eggs.

2

A design a sign a finger

old lady someone's old finger

that points to another finger that is pointing that is pointing up

someone's old finger doesn't point to a brown-haired girl

brown-haired and brown-eyed

fist around pestle

thumb fingers of left hand holding silver mortar still

old lady someone's leathery old finger

that points to another finger that is pointing

finger of Jesus another finger

pointing up

someone else in the kitchen with two other women

Jesus

in the kitchen with brown-haired girl with old lady someone

with Mary of Bethany and with Martha.

3

Finger old lady someone's old finger

to finger

another that is pointing that is pointing up

finger to finger

from finger to finger line of the word stretched tight a tight rope

tight rope in the kitchen with a brown-haired girl

brown-haired and brown-eyed

disinclined to move

fingers around pestle thumb fingers holding silver mortar

silver mortar reflecting brown table

one of two other women Mary of Bethany

doing the one thing

no clothes on

doing the shake on down line of the word stretched tight

on a tight rope in the kitchen.

4

Someone's in the kitchen with a brown-haired girl

old lady someone's finger to finger that is pointing up

from finger to finger line of the word stretched tight a tight rope

two other women in the kitchen

Mary and Martha

Mary's doing the shake on a tight rope in the kitchen

brown-haired girl disinclined

fingers around pestle holding silver mortar still on the table

garlic clove red pepper on the brown table

plate of four fish

brown and black pitcher

one of two women Martha in a blonde wig

doing the other thing needful finger-pop in a corner of the kitchen

in a gold lamé sheath

it's finger it's finger-popping time in the kitchen.

Call

In what memory as a stream carries along

and without announcement

announces

a sort of resurfacing

coming up to the surface of what is not memory

in the middle of memory and habit

out of memory and habit and desire in the middle of the day

and not a matter of words and thus almost frightening

as what announces without announcement

is frightening

slightest ripple slightest swirl

no more than a moment a moment of silence over the telephone

as the cards say

of "deepest sympathy."

Pastorelle 7

Mud along the edge of the creek

creek or small river

and low during the summer

low water and increased edge of mud rank smell

in the heat

many rocks exposed slick to touch

the problem is not finding a rock there are

many

the problem is not turning

into a rock

the problem is a problem of how

far how far can I throw myself and how far can I

throw myself again.

Rhythm and Blues Singer

1

Dead in January in Memphis

James Carr

rhythm and blues singer

who never learned to read or write

superior

so superior to Bartleby who failed to unlearn reading and writing

sever the ties that bind

words entangle us

words in letters of the alphabet the letters in written words

rhythm = the backbeat of all biological pleasures

blues = bad luck and trouble

to sing is to be untied.

2

Language before writing

before reading

before the alphabet

acoustic

river

a river of sound

river

a river of action

charm and more than charm

conferred by sound

action

for survival

what to do

how to

do

what to do.

3

Language after writing

after reading

after the alphabet

visual

signs no wonders

silent in

silent lines

silent signs in silent lines

for argument

a river silenced and

straightened

syllogism

one line

all men are mortal

James Carr is a man

another.

4

Dark

tangled and entangled at the dark end of the street

a you and a me

an us like Pierre and Isabel

readers

readers and writers and lovers

found going to be found entangled in the letters in written words in

the invention of romance

song of the rhythm and blues singer

who couldn't read or write nor could survive

mortality

could   care   less.

The Compulsion to Repeat

1

Gradually how gradually

one comes to understand the poets

as gradually as

the compulsion of one's own compulsion the compulsion to repeat

expense of

spirit

waste of shame

one who lives in terms of trees

who thinks of the bride while he works in/among trees

solitary work with metal tools and metal machines

not a mythological love of a mythological god.

2

That spirit

is the imagination

inner life and private life

a life of images of images of what cannot be in one's life

that shame is modesty

that images are expensive that one's life is spent

keeping images to oneself that one's life is wasted in this keeping

one who lives in terms of trees

thinks of the bride while he works with tools and machines

not one of the photographed white women

of the image of the bride.

Pastorelle 8

Young woman

Amish

green dress black apron translucent white prayer bonnet

strings of her bonnet trailing in the air

rollerskating down the road

by herself alone in the air and light of an ungloomy Sunday afternoon

herself and her skating shadow

the painter said

beauty is what we add to things

and I

chainsawing in the woods above the road

say what could be added

what other than giving this roaring machine a rest.

Moonrise

Two

day being over shadows

across

pale and luminous and nonsymbolic moon rises

one of the two = the number 9

a miracle according to the first poet to write from experience

the other = a number with a shoulder

two

on a country road at moonrise.

At the Counters Ball

Last dance a waltz jazzed up slowed

down out of time real easy is in three played free

and so all the time in the world

last dance for the counters it's the last dance at the counters ball

a waltz for the counters who've spent all their time counting

what's lost like

things like favorite things not things

like time

after the ball is over back in their counting houses

the counters will be counting what's lost

and all the counters are laughing because I asked Emily "do I repeat

myself" and she said "but very well" and they're dancing

because they've lost count and

don't care and because it's the last

dance and I'm dancing

laughing and dancing with the oh so divine Miss Emily D.

Car Museum

1

These are the cars

Auburns and Cords and Duesenbergs

rare

machines of rare elegance

and this is back home in Indiana

rare

inexplicable

museum once showroom and factory headquarters

on a small-town street like the streets

where I grew up runaway tramp and young rebel gentleman from Indiana

from small towns like this town

or from interruptions or from small interruptions in the fields

flatness of the fields

hadn't remembered this intolerable flatness.

2

Candy apple Auburn 852 Speedster

the grille shield-shaped slightly tilted back not Achilles' shield

tilted back into long level line of the hood

chrome exhaust coils

coming out each side

of the hood

room for only two behind the grille the hood the coils

grape-colored Cord 812 Beverly Sedan

headlights concealed

in S-curve fenders sticking out

from the raked body curved aerodynamic voluptuously aerodynamic

black Duesenberg J Murphy Torpedo Convertible Coupe

abrupt leaving

least

abrupt pointed stern

black torpedo boat leaving least detectable wake

in the sea of love or country road after dark.

3

Without memory there is no protection

from the flatness of all the fields undeniable unanticipated

intolerable

no longer a boy or young man

from somewhere else who had to go somewhere else had to and

has to

away from the fields

inexplicable not in a

chapter in the glossy-paper chapters of arts and ideas

Indiana can be explained

the cars cannot

perhaps elegance can never be explained

boy or young man hadn't known the cars weren't on the streets then

perhaps rebellion is the unknowing pursuit of elegance.

4

From "Indiana" to "Donna Lee"

to a woman change of the jazz musician

the chord changes don't change and

faster with more notes

the history of jazz is faster and faster with more notes on the changes

that don't change

faster with more notes becomes a blurring into

a woman

pure articulation of a woman

lonely woman

pure articulation of the blues which is pure loneliness

which don't change go faster go further go away oh so far as far away

end up lonely

James Dean ended up lonely from Indiana and ended up lonely

my hero

gone

in a car not one of the elegant cars.

Parmenides/Fragments 3 and 15a

1

To think = to be

statement needing to become

image

you will come to know what you think although not when you see

what you say

when you see what it is that you are doing

most gradual of images.

2

Word in the Greek in itself unbroken needing nothing

hudatorizon

rooted-in-water.

3

Conodoguinet small

river locally a creek many turnings

boundary of what the map says is mine

boundary to the west to the middle of its turning bed which remains

undredged

muddy

containing stones ripple

slide of water low because of the heat/drought ripple and slide

around stones

no one kind various colors several shapes

pulled out

hauled away to make not quite regular irregular steps.

4

On each side roses

carrying buckets of water two at a time scent of roses

there can be no argument against penetration.

5

Effort to balance some effort to climb more or less level steps

pause before climbing

down

whole stretch of the mountain mass

and line ridge line of north mountain massive and elongated blue wave

what

I do what I think

climbing up and climbing down.

Pastorelle 14

1

Ramps Bridge named

after Jacob or named after ford on the creek or

small river also named after Jacob

no longer here when the bridge was built

1882

migrant in the great migration Indiana Kansas Missouri finally Oregon

proof you can leave your mark

if you leave

and if you're remembered.

2

Saved from quaintness from the antique the "collectible"

by use still in use the plank runners worn smooth

by traffic.

3

Use = noise

cars burning rubber squeals and shouting of passengers horns honking

how to know a covered bridge is still in use = noise.

4

Reasons for covering bridges

to keep water out of the joints to keep the roadway dry

strengthen the structure

to make the bridge look like a barn to horses

not to frighten the horses to keep

snow off

to provide darkness

for those seeking light the light shining best after darkness after

a not overly long rite/ritual of initiation in darkness.

5

The structure = the truss principle

which = all parts

of the bridge connected by a series of triangles

one post leaning against

another series of one against another each connected at the top and

the bottom by beams the beams are called chords

the structure = the truss principle + arch

the arch in sections

pinned/bolted to the posts upright posts of the triangles

and this is marvelous

connected

the wooden arch connected to the wooden triangles

and this is marvelous this is the mystery what really matters

the structure is

what matters the flower the music of it.

6

1991 the bridge on fire

extinguished just in time by my neighbor running out in the night

relieved a woman said "the bridge is all we've got."

7

Reasons for burning covered bridges

to protest love lack

of love lack of a love letter left in secret in the structure

to protest prince and princess

who sing operatically they've found truth and love die Wahrheit and

love after a not overly long rite/ritual of initiation

mystery the mystery of the

structure to protest building of the structure

over the mystery of the unbuilt of the structureless creek or small river.

8

The plank runners two

of them three boards wide the boards nailed

to the deck planking the nail heads themselves worn smooth by traffic

higher

than the deck can be difficult to stay on the runners in the dark

it's always dark inside a covered bridge

can be accidents can be collisions

with the posts with mystery

in the dark.

9

1804 Theodore Burr patented the truss principle + arch

like Mozart

buried in an unmarked grave.

Pastorelle 15

The Chinese

in the drought of 1876–1879 reportedly confused

rustling of dry leaves for rain

when the ear's not yet adulterated/unadulterated in the morning

late at night or very early in the morning

it sounds like rain.

Kitaj Dancer

Without pretext

the pretext of a text

any costume that comes with the pretext of a text

wears only warm-up leggings

and so thighs that do work pubic smudge unsequined ribs + breasts

a big girl

big/grown-up/adult in expectation the expectation of movement

unthematic/semplice/in itself and so outside of memory

stands doesn't stand on her head stands smallest smile

exquisite

the phrase incomplete no quotation marks.

Why Trees Weep

Because they're listening to Sainte Colombe's "Les Pleurs"

because those they would love don't

love them flee

from them

because their neighbors are beset with illness/disease experience

pain in movement or

can't move can only sit in gardens going to weeds

Niobe lost all her children.

Plinth

Broken

cannot be glued cannot be pinned

what can be done = the parts abutted

bolting them

to the rough foundation stones from the old schoolhouse

the plinth resting on/bolted to those stones

what can be done

that music may enter as through a welcoming portal may enter this

air/among these pines.

There Are Birds

2008

Refrains for Robert Quine

Love comes in spurts.

RICHARD HELL & THE VOIDOIDS

1

And goes is gone

cause for mourning head

in hands in tears gonna be a long long wait for the resurrection

of the dead.

There are birds there is birdsong

unmourning and unmournful at sunrise in the white light

there is a garden with high walls around it

jardin de plaisir

of mint and lavender of hyssop in hedges glassy beads of water on velvet leaves

purple-flaked lupin spikes above velvet pulmonaria

there is a gardener la belle jardinière bare-breasted and bare-footed

bouquets

of all flowers in her arms and woven in her hair.

2

And it hurts not good but

bad

to see a man head in hands in tears it breaks you up

to see a man come down in tears.

There are birds there is birdsong

having come through hunger and danger

there is free song

a free weaving of many songs

song against song and other songs clustered/spun out in a blending of wavy pitches

tant

doucement the phrase means what the songs mean

freshness

that meaning so sweetly and freely as a gardener weaves flowers in her hair.

3

Can we stay in the weave of

that meaning can we/should we attempt to stay to linger

in a pleasure garden everlasting dream of

love tomorrow its unseen/secret structure when our time remains a

bad time and what time wasn't

bad

wasn't and isn't a time of hunger and danger of young men and older men

in tears our time a time

of terror and counterterror can

we/should

we our

time remaining a really bad time a really down and dirty time

of terror what

walls do not fall and who says they have no fear.

4

And boo-hoo-hoo

like dolls

hurts breaks you up like dolls get broken the visible human

the visibly spastic plastic.

There are birds there is birdsong

unmourning and unmournful having come through

there is a garden with swept gravel paths

dream designed/bel et bon designed connecting and interconnecting

non brisé

where men and women are in contemplation in conversation in

one another's eyes

there is a gardener holding her bouquets and holding her skirts like the light like

so sweetly woven song like love never for sale.

Odor of Quince

1

As sound it's Lester it's Lester Young returned/never gone leaping in but

gently

gentle tongue on the reed

in rapport with the body of the note

warm and tender enough body as if that body were about to awaken

an arm unwound a leg unbent

as if curve of the arm as if curve of the leg were about to become one curve

a sigh

from an about to awaken recumbent body

there must be a French word for it

because the note's one note one and only long opening sigh note of a French tune

désinvolture

tongue on that word ribbon-candy contour of its vowels

given extension/extending without constraint

beats forgotten bar lines forgotten

even Agnes Martin's shy/gossamer graph paper pencil lines curve

of the note extended going and going and beyond all that

gently warmly tenderly without lack of purpose purposive purposively

not the swirl of a stern Pompeian matron's mantle or

Judith Jamison's slow fan skirt or the peacock display/flourishment of Johnny Hodges

this is Lester Young in rapport and ardemment

and this is one note long opening sigh

note then three notes

a triplet broken up each note stepped/spaced out a body's three exhalations

they fall away from the sigh of the one note

leaves from a tree in

late October/November

or one leaf which is the number 3 combined with that same number

but backwards

one leaf seen three ways

seen from one side from the other the other number 3

seen together/horizontally flagrant

lips

cascade/descent/glide of the notes like a song

Lester singing with Lady Day singing "Fine and Mellow" singing belle

et moelleuse

three notes which fall away in

their own curve

these three exhalations giving articulation to the given extension

then harp-tone/vibraphone glissandos

up and down the horn

in layers and layers chains of frills in the sashay of goldfish tails a loose/déshabillé

fabric

on which is scattered a scattered florilège of inflorescences/flowers without names

simple stars

in a repeat/no repeat Moroccan rhythm getting quiet

getting quieter microtonal flowers and stars between repeat/

no repeat rests until the air itself breathes with a repeat/no repeat breath.

2

As color considered as a car a pink Cadillac

customized

the whole thing taken apart/stripped down to the essential torse/torso

where the car came from the luxe calme and volupté junkyard

where the job gets done where else it can only be

Rothko's body shop

a long job it takes a careful kind of character you have to know what you're doing

careful and serious

twenty-three coats of pink is serious

one after or on another one coat which is lightly sanded/hand-rubbed another

coat lightly sanded/hand-rubbed

twenty-three coats

a long job it takes time for a coat to dry

you have to take a break take your time step back sit down have a smoke you have to think about it

if

it's to be not "like new" but new

but a new vehicle of transport and delight

and not Renoir's rosy-cheeked bather or Matisse's

rosy all over/flamingo chaise longue chaise lounge easy chair

or de Kooning's woman with a hat a wet-on-wet cherry jubilee cake frosting skirt

if it's to be

a new vehicle no chrome

pink after or on participial pink

each coat thin as a film a film that's been diluted

with solvent

pigment particles almost disassociated from the film barely clinging

to the surface that's been sanded/hand-rubbed when light hits the particles

it bounces back suffusing the surface which is twenty-three surfaces which are

becoming no surface/light

becoming the emergent impingement of pink light itself

a long job and

risky it's risky to ignore the limits of

physical coherence a Cadillac car the female form the chemistry of paint

it's risky to take apart/strip down

to ignore to take leave of/walk away from

all that's been loved and to leave pink light all by itself

which needs some blue

some blue underlining as a barre for a dancer to help make stable what cannot

be stable/is motile to help give some arabesque/Arabian motility to the motility

which needs a fresco a whole wall of purple which

comes from an oasis an orchard dream trunks and tree branches

along a path a stream

the trees are porches/portals a parade approaching a parenthetical moon

there's a body

empurpled nymph body on a cloth of gold

white gold

that is the ripeness of all that is ripeness that is the empurpled key to the dream

and to the

whole adamant mood of a fresco a wall

which makes the impingement more than an impingement

giving it drama ballets and divertissements depths and subtleties sensual

summonings.

3

As sign apprehended a new sign carved

by a tramp

a person who tramps/moves about "le voyageur fondamental"

fundamentally a gypsy surviving like a gypsy surviving

though no thief of

chickens or of children

like old Schimmel the woodcarver though

unbearded not an aesthetical beard communing with nature/windchime

pines to commune with a convex/so complex self

not a noble scholar beard on a leopard-skin rug collating "rainy" words all

in a row or an heroical beard

astride a craggy promontory confronting ocean spray/the spraying surf in a suit

a tramp a person recognizable from childhood a childhood snapshot

blanket over his shoulder tied with binder-twine among taller than him dusty hollyhocks

what a gypsy a tramp who has nothing has

an animal alertness to signs to changes in the weather what's
in the air

what a gypsy a tramp a carver
does carves

what's in the air makes room/space for what will be a new sign in the air

one and only long opening sigh
body's
exhalations
harp-tone/vibraphone glissandos chains of frills inflorescences
flowers simple
stars in a repeat/no repeat Moroccan rhythm
pink needing some blue
not little girl blue on a fresco a whole wall of purple an oasis an orchard dream
slumbering empurpled body a dream a mood

a structure of mood

depths and subtleties summonings

emerging from that structure from a more than emergent pink impingement

what a carver does

carves "from nature" a likeness thinks about it takes his

time many mornings perhaps years

carves again the work of a moment after many mornings/years

Mr. Johnson the pipemaker said his hands went so fast he didn't know what

they were doing

directement/straight

into sounds colors makes room/space for and makes a new sign the

shadow of

of what was given to him

in his voyaging/moving about of the shadow of a

smile

what a carver a gypsy a tramp does leaves

a given for what was given a new sign immediate and intimate and though
no thief or shepherd either and must be/is moving on.

Grey Scale/Zukofsky

1

To become aware of tones

beginner's problem in the mind of the beginner

visualization of white of whiteness

which is impossible

I saw an egret in a scraggly cedar above

Big Spring

Williams said no whiteness is so white as the memory of whiteness

in a cedar or motionless in water/the tall grasses.

2

Silver maple woods what Jennifer named

the scary woods

scary so dense and so dark

dense with undergrowth

with heaped-up multiflora rose with jewelweed

damselfly

a or the or neither and darker than

dark

black wings at rest on jewelweed blackness without dots or density.

3

Middle grey

sledgehammer

to break up cast-iron machines

bow saw to cut down weedy box elders shot up around the machines

time

in which to make a cleared space to find limestone/middle grey

Pound said wind is part of the process

rain part of the process.

4

Three tones + other tones

glaring surface of snow in flat sunlight it's white it's a white world willful travelers

without colored and coloring glasses

long gone

snow in full shade

white with delicate textures sand dune ripples any Bach fugue

average snow

average white skin the shadow of a dolphin

leaves of trees their shadows

no snow

dark material dark fur dark grey cat named Friendly.

Three tones + other tones + two tones

Richard Avedon's 1958 photograph of Pound a postcard a bookmark

darker closed

eyes wrinkled texture of sagging skin around eyes

and darker closed lips no texture almost no-tone tone

"but shall have his sorrow for

sea-fare"

two tones

first suggestions/thresholds of his sorrow.

6

The great photographs are black and white and middle grey

Weston

at Point Lobos rock solid shadow of eroded

rock

Ansel Adams at Yosemite and

elsewhere morning star aspen leaves

Stieglitz portraits of Georgia O'Keeffe not simply not necessarily great

not because of subject matter this is the American

earth and personages.

7

The great

result of reduction and the composition of reduction

resulting in intensity Williams

said the only human value = intense

intense face of sorrow

on a postcard

although there are other emotions and although there are other

faces.

8

And so I come

to the

to the one/only photograph on my wall

and am I not one of those travelers a willful one or merely a stubborn one

still stubborn still

come

home to Ralph Eugene Meatyard's 1968 photograph of Zukofsky

on my wall.

9

No eyes/closed eyes

behind large dark glasses darker than leaves of trees their shadows larger

made larger/darker by wings/rock eyebrows

the mouth is also closed

unsmiling

face

to shadow face

large on a neck of average white skin.

10

No face = no image = no memory

eyes + mouth + what's been overlooked/unremembered

beginner's error

+ an ear for instance

image of intense attention

what I remember = "only song matters"

not one song only but one/only photograph

on my wall.

11

Call it a cadenza/some traveling music

off the scale

and going/getting past the question of who's the fairest of them all

of them all watching over me

after a or the or

neither.

Show and Tell/Robert Creeley

Aspen the

'60s

where/when everything happened the beginning

when I first heard Coltrane

and saw something

Bobby Byrd said it was a good poem he was from Memphis and ought to know

when a gamine-faced girl came running from an airplane with her arms

outstretched

this is me then young man young poet

beside the Roaring Fork or a tributary the open blue and white *For Love* book in

one hand

the other in a gesture of appeal

the assignment show and tell show what

you love

this poem "A Song"

fine clockwork of it subtle grammar of it of its words

their sounds and arrayment

Monk/Mozart refinement of the shifting pitches of this poem all fitted together

quiet and

quiet

and unheard/cannot be heard over the white noise steady roar of the churned

up white water

hear me now all these years later

having spent the years in the song in the song/life business

having

paid dues

reading with older/different eyes

which see what they see through/after tears the locked the unacknowledged

unlocked

it is the learning of the meaning of the blues

help you see something see something you didn't see before

which is what is wanted in this poem which is a song and what the several

requirements are

a grace

a song requires a girl so bright/in bloom who rejoices the heart to whom one

gives gifts gives a diversity of gifts

a sign

the life of which is its use

which is Wittgenstein's *The Blue & Brown Books* which was our conversation then

Toby

and I when I arrived/right off

the bus young men on unpaved/dirt streets of the silver town

the life of which

is its use as adornment a gift among a diversity of gifts

a poet's thinking the long labor with words

the tenses

want wanted have/had wanted not what a young man was so wanting and wanting

but what a

song wants just a few a spoonful of the right the rough and the smooth words in the right order here and

there a rest making room for breath and letting a few of the words sink in

careful/with care how a song is to be sung if one sings it and

the last of the requirements

for *care is clear* having come through the ambiguities/tears having had to learn the

meaning

of the blues

what will fit on a bracelet a simple inscription

all these years later

hear me now having stepped back and needing to come forward

this poem is a song an

act

a work of love.

New Work

2010

Kitaj Angels

Before she left for her own studio each day,
Sandra used to remind me to put the music on.

R.B. KITAJ

1

Big wings lots of colors

red blue green yellow a pale purple

iris within the colors

raised "fall" of the iris which is saying it with a flower

saying

she angel

splotches/stains on her she angel body

choppy waves around/behind her body terrene and marine angel with

flowered eyes

fruit/fruitlike + pink berry breasts on not-level table dreaming

parts of her dream being split open being bulbs

unrolled neon candlelike red thing two-in-one thing candlelike and the

hectic on her cheek

bird in flight in her dream.

Also big also lots

red blue green no yellow and mottled "with mottles
rare" mottled
with black

shapes one of the shapes of power big snake shape him not slim

angel
he angel with an orange ball-peen
hammer head now there's some power for you

his strider leg
also splotches/stains but lighter but ochre but kind of pink on his strider
leg under the table

he is leaning over her from the other side of the table he
is leaning over her dream
eye-patched eye he is listening to "the music" he is
listening to bird in flight the song of
that bird.

She angel dreaming

he angel leaning over her dream

lutes being old

Fender electric bass slight

sustain on duuum on single duuum   duuums

cloud phases scanty pedal steel underlinings along the way

bird in flight music

the music and the words to the music

the words are imploring words imploring where my love might be is there

someone waiting where and is

there the words go on they don't/won't stop

imploring

if you like adjectives it's "wonderful" and "crazy" and "sad" finally

let's face it "American"

dreaming

leaning over her dream.

In the realm/region of the

possible of possibility and anxiety because

of possibility

hand

in his he angel hand

realm/region of snow in which huddled cattle freeze in

which two travelers may get lost may

lose one another call and call and call again to one another

hand bones connected to arm bones arm in arm one long all connected arm

bone ochre kind of pink suffused

realm/region of

feedback

crackles grainy buzz/fuzz

feedback after there is silence and there is seven times silence

she is dreaming he is leaning/listening she and he who are one arm

are ochre kind of pink exploit in the white exploit of snow.

You're together, you're touching, and yet you both have wings. If you remain together, you'll never be able to use your wings. They are really quite splendid. There are people who would pay good money for wings like that. Still, why have splendid wings if you're not going to use them?

Yes, you can fly together, but won't you always be bumping against one another, colliding? Do you have insurance?

And what if each of you has to fly in a different direction? I mean each of you as separate in a separate direction. Just sometimes, every now and then and not for very long, a day or two or several days in succession. For appointments, separate appointments.

What are days or time zones to angels, anyway?

2

Curvilinear

lower than longer than the angels

austere body ghost body

a bounded writhing

a bounded bride a wraith and her wreath together become something becoming

linear

her raised arm and her wreath together becoming curved

and linear

lower than longer than ghost body barely

there at

the margin of what's there marginal remainder of what had been known

austere body bleached brown ghost

body

barely and becoming the embodiment of what had been known.

Try-on not so big wings fewer

colors

one yellow red orange wing brushing/bent by

curvilinear something

and drooping zipper stuck/not zipped up

banana split maraschino cherry face "the face is the soul of the

body"

soul of the body banana split soul

the body is a baby angel/angel baby body a doo-wop little darling a premodern

Olympia prompting pantomimic gestures and so fine angel

baby body

let the they say say what they say about going steady

what a body says

come is what an angel body says and is saying come and go with me

other wing not zipped up

here and there snow on the body.

Fewer two is

fewer one red + one green one

red light green light not so big "bequest" of wings

Michelangeloesque angel downsized

white beard faith of our fathers Moses/before Ray Charles beard

snowman eye he's looking up he's looking

her over and seeing something else something going linear

what had been known

what had been known

what hadn't been known hadn't been enough known as the earth had

not

got a stop or go problem he's

got an eye

problem a division of vision he's got one of those der Abschied problems

stop/linger awhile with what had been known or come/go/move on up a little

higher the empyrean which could be maybe heaven.

Left/left out surface part of the surface seen from

above an airplane

looking down from an airplane

seen through clouds rumpled sheets

sweet thing and white beard angel bodies

on the clouds not so big/smaller bodies they look smaller they have smaller

wings

here and there snow on their bodies they look precarious their

wings look precarious

so stricken so severe face/surface of the earth part of it

austere

bare

barely there

known not known

enough surface of what had not been known left/left out/outside the

years the weather.

MEDITATION

You're not touching. You're not together, not so much together.

You're playing chicken. That's what the two of you are doing, two angels who are playing chicken. You're getting ready to depart for separate appointments in separate directions. You're getting ready, and you're hesitating. A hesitation waltz. You want to see who departs first, becomes disappeared first. Who cries and who pushes who toward the door. You want to see who cries out please don't go first.

3

Bigger perhaps the biggest

wings green yellow jukebox colors but subdued

in the down position

no need to go anywhere the "scarlet experiment" concluded nothing left to

prove

would bleed would die she would

after death and transfiguration there's nothing left to

prove

she angel body transfigured snow angel body some spots/

splotches but subdued on her

snow angel body

one black breast abrupt fruit black fruit

something of the marine remaining/mermaid's offering it is her

gift.

Bigger perhaps the biggest

wings fewest colors no perhaps about it

one is fewest black

is fewest

white beard grown longer a projective a projectile beard war memorial shell casing

painted white still to be seen right here/right now/today in America

pale iris color but not an iris a bellflower projected

bellflower's stamen projected

no need to run from town to town

no need to run away from he angel's nodding pale flower his

gift

many and more recent spots/splotches on his he angel

body bulked up altogether more resolute

he angel body after death and transfiguration he angel snow angel body

more recent snow angel

more recently with nothing to prove.

What does Maimonides say

Maimonides says angel means messenger

two snow angels one

message she and he arm in arm

who are one long arm no longer ochre kind of pink suffused who are one long

arm all grimed with one color a grave color black color

the message is not a mixed message is not a seduction a come a little

closer vampire/vampirella message the message is

waiting's over

is an I and a Thou or Thee may be

dancers unmasked and face to face that it is permitted that an I and a Thou or Thee

may be in one another's eyes

may share "the privilege"

two

having nothing to prove

aren't in confrontation are in conversation.

This is paradise

to be in

to be in the place where conversation takes place

could be a garden could be within a wall

could be two who are face to face who are within a wall

of gold

who are not in with the in crowd

could be exuberant/protuberant flowers a palm tree passion flowers in passion

air

unseen birds their song of songs in the air

and what it may be asked what is the tenor/the tone of their conversation

perhaps the ruby tone of "dear" or "my dear" perhaps

forgiveness

in speech under speech the air and the birds left undisturbed

perhaps forgiveness

this is paradise to be in the place where conversation takes place.

You're back together. You're back in touch and touching. You're arm in arm. You're hand in hand. I can't tell where your hands begin and end. Why is your long arm so black? It wasn't black before, but now it's all black.

And why are you bleeding? Because it isn't enough to be arm in arm? You're bleeding. It looks like a red river coming out of you. Bright, then darker, scarlet. You want him to see a red river and sit by your side. You want him to love you again.

Won't you die, won't you be a dead angel? Won't you die before he sits by your side and loves you again?

4

One and

only one wing

red green yellow streamer colors

bent streamer dangling from handlebar of crashed motor/machine

there's been an accident

she angel her body on top of he angel body pileup

two who were in conversation in conversation no more

two who tried to take a ride who tried to be closer than just a little bit closer

two almost/not quite content

close can be too close

her angel eyes and her angel face

smeared

blue blue blue mascara/marmalade face

the report would say this is a stuck together forever pileup a wreck.

Almost no wings amputated/remnant

wing is almost no

he angel with

dangling/hanging down arm no longer arm in arm

no longer one long arm

all grimed with a grave color

dangling/hanging down arm that's been burned that's

spotted/splotched with crash and burn colors

+ shrunken Michelangeloesque/Popeye the Sailor Man arm

+ no face

where his he angel face should be there's a phallus a look at that

mushroom head on its jammed gear-shifter stalk

a phallus a microphone picking

up what's in the air after crash and burn a pileup a wreck what's between

red and white

not fade not fade away no no never pink noise in pink air.

What causes crash and burn a wreck

driving under the influence

does

the influence of a can't get no satisfaction picture

large of

a large bather standing in a yearning posture in water in cotton

candy waterfall water

another large bather leaning against a tree the tree is leaning out over a

waterfall branches of the tree

are leaning out over a waterfall yearningly

two bather bodies separated by bodies j'regret bodies same old same old six

of separation

got a picture on the brain look out where you're going

yearning to come closer to become

one

embraceable I embraceable Thou or Thee one.

What's in the air after crash and burn pileup/wreck

what's in the air

after there's been an accident

what's between scarlet experiment and snow

not fade not fade away pink noise of one word the one word

"wish"

the one word and its

exposition

which exposes "wish you were here"

modulating and modulating very slowly the particles pink particles

within the supposedly single/cries alone syllable noise

wah-wah particle and the breath/barely breathing particle skidding into the hit

come to a halt particle

the last at last hushed particle

pink particles modulating very slowly modulating into a measure a ring

and is ringing.

MEDITATION

You're leaning on him, you're all over him. You could smother that
he angel! You wanted him to sit by your side and stay by your side.
Like a wedding of two old people who get married sitting down.

Old people have brown spots on their hands and white hair. They
get married for "companionship." My mother told me that.

You're anxious he doesn't hasten to bid you adieu. You're anxious
about companionship and adieu.

5

Straight

a straight and a narrow a black

line

on one side of/behind the line a list of names

in black and white in

sans-serif type the severest of them all

names and straight up and down marks the names of the in crowd severest

crowd of a ruler

which measures who's out of line who's been caught in the act of

making

any likeness of anything

in heaven above in the earth beneath in the water under the earth

anything like the figure the human angel she the

human angel he figure.

What rules the ruler lays down

the law

is not golden

is high up in black/lights out letters flat black on

white letters

one of those old thou shall not laws the non figuratif one

what rules the ruler

truck-stop sign somewhere in the Midwest high above that wide landscape

rolling and tumbling toward the plains

so high you can't get over it is higher/

highest above just about

everything

old as Moses/before Ray Charles above that wide landscape

that rolling and tumbling toward part of the surface

what rules the ruler

black on white.

There's been a change

of wings

one vermilion wing for him one pale yellow

wing for her

there's been a change of scene of what's to be seen under the truck-stop sign

at the drive-in a double feature featuring a him and a her

no voice-over of snow over

bones wispy bits of hair no more snow scenes it's "The Creative Act"

rated "R" for recreational/revelational

for the perplexed

unperplexes shows what to do

with love's convenient things what to do with hands what hands

can do

her warmly kind of pink arm ending in a brush

she's giving him excitations he's feeling good vibrations

he's feeling not dead but brand-new.

What hands can do

his pink human he angel arm ending

in a curved scepter a stamen a bellflower's projecting brush

projecting

power

rebel rebel power to make a human she angel yellow

she's yellow all over she's got yellow hips that won't quit she's a yellower

yellow all over

"one can't have too much"

no way she's some

dark sonnet lady/queen of the nightmare scene a shadowy sphinx woman in the sun

so the perplexed will

will please get the picture of what hands can

do

they can hold hands they can make

you feel not dead but living transfigured and bright/brand-new.

MEDITATION

You were sick with an infection of the throat and mouth. Feverish. Your gums hurt, you had trouble swallowing. She visited you when you were sick. She helped you swallow. There was touching, there was more touching, and you got excited. Although you were sick, feverish, you got excited. Admit it. Some things can't be hidden under a green blanket.

Then she left, had other visits on her schedule. What did you expect? A visiting nurse angel always has other visits on her schedule.

And now look at you. You're making a doll. Large, larger than life, painted yellow. Since when do she angel dolls wear bikinis? Besides, she's topless and you forgot her head. I think you've got the worried life blues. You're worried about her. You're worried she's not worried about you. You're not in her head or only just a little. She left. Didn't leave a trinket, some smallest small thing. If other angels see your doll, they'll say that's voodoo, that's crazy like Kokoschka. They'll have you put away. They'll say you're "touched."

Crazy old angel.

Crazy old angel come down with those worried life blues.

6

Been a change a change of position

an act

an assumption

coming down to gather to lift

there's an obligation that comes with the assumption of an act of assumption

an obligation to lift up

one flame stained

+ one orange hammer wing in intervention

in the power glide position a fire-maker a carrier of warmth

he angel with the power to act/to do what love is not supposed to be

able to do

to gather to lift a she angel gone cold

from that wider than wide landscape that

realm/region of snow.

Hot or not

either you are or you're not she angel's not is

cold

one all bright as blood wing which is swelling/swollen a hindered

flag a not so funny valentine

disease resulting in death is not so funny

heart disease Miranda

disease of suffering with those you see suffer of being touched of your heart

going out to those you see suffering

piteous/pietà heart going out to and getting out of whack

what she saw

amber-colored bird American

bird cowboyish eagle riding high in the saddle

brought down/ambushed by the stones of the stone-throwing crowd

it is no secret what stones can do can bring a bird

down.

Dying at her music

ritardando and ritardando and then the no/no more/nothing

ritardando

she angel her arm/hand hanging down white

kind of blue in the dying and then the

dead position

she's dead forget the feather

he angel in intervention in the hoodoo/who do you love position

Jim Dandy angel to the

rescue

up and down chicken scratch slow gain/sustain slow but gentle burn

his he angel hand on the strings of her all rounded back bikini yellow jazz guitar

lutes being old mandolins having been banished

not dead white and not any kind of blue and not ascenseur pour l'échafaud

inner mounting

flame rose pink shading to deep tremolo purple.

Poor Moses

poor old sprechstimme stutterer

tongue-tied in his before Ray Charles beard

can't stand it won't let himself look won't let himself listen

to sight also sound of what love is not

supposed to be able

to do the going all the way going all out/for broke gathering and lifting up

sight of a human he angel with the power to act/to do

body and soul music sound

poor Moses

got a mono/monotonous picture of no picture/an idea on the brain

an idea

of an idea no worte und no bilder

poor old baseball manager who can't stand it

the rules the commandments of the game done been changed

who's been left holding a heart-shaped stone.

MEDITATION

She's dying all over again. She's sitting in a sprawled-out sort of way and dying. Or she's sitting, and she's already dead.

She could be sleeping. She could be playing dead. Children know that, after they die, people will be nice. It's what happens at funerals. They will say they miss them. They miss them, they hold them in their hearts, and they promise to stop saying things that hurt. Things that hurt in crow voices. It's easy. All you have to do is die, and they will stop. Then they will sing the song about the circle and bye and bye.

If she's dying or already dead, if she's sleeping or playing dead, what are you going to do? Will you come near and say very quietly time to wake up, beautiful girl?

Or will you say angels who die before they wake are lucky?

Will you sit by her side?

7

Having come so far the location and the condition of

where angels are

life/later than death location and condition of

where two angels are

the "utter simplicity" of what is there where two human angels are

by true

negatives some slantwise similar

dissimilarities

like the Hollywood hills for instance

conflagration/conglomeration of orange red floriation + brown dark matter

floriation over long and low rise + speed bumps of the hills

somewhere there's a wide-screen TV

big rock melted candy mountain + bluebird of happiness on the screen

somewhere there's a pool.

Like two heads after the party for instance

can get loud party somewhere in the Hollywood hills

in that landscape which is a conglomeration of floriations + wide screen +

pool

that landscape which is subject to heaving to shaking to a

whole lot of shaking going on

head to head open mouth

to open mouth at a careful distance

from each mouth little orange red and dark matter souvenirs

little souvenirs and

a pattern and a pillow of broken threads the little souvenirs make a

parallelogram

boogie-woogie parallelogram between two mouths at a very careful distance

is after

is much later

this is after the party's over.

Where

and how two angels are

forget the negatives forget the dissimilarities

no motel no shadows where

they are these

two who are lighted signs in walking something having been given/given up

to get something you have to give something up

small blue sailboat

sail one small wing remaining

no need/necessity to fly higher having been lifted and

launched

she face

shekhina face having been surprised by this could be joy and launched

she's a sail on honeybee

face and

snow white human she angel body lit up with light/yellow.

She angel

sailing on walking and leading the way

he angel one

stained wing remaining

no need/necessity to fulfill further obligations of further assumptions

these two walking/going their going/going together

in rhythm

in Ernest Ranglin reggae grooving rhythm

they have easy going feet

their going/going together is not

on assumptions but on the fact that this must/can only be Eden

simplicity of their condition which is love/life later than

death

the utter simplicity of their location which is

Eden

a he and a she who are as they are who are signs lit up with light/yellow.

You've solved the problem with splendid wings and different directions. The one wing each solution. One each, each a little less splendid. Smaller.

You're walking. You're not climbing ladders. That's what the two of you are doing, two angels who are walking together.

It's the music, isn't it? Someone changed the music. Or the music changed itself like the sky changes itself. So it doesn't have to be the same music over and over. Pulse and throb, parched and plangent trumpet echo against pulse and throb is the same over and over. The sky changes. Doesn't have to be the same. Not even bird in flight, the song of that bird. Doesn't have to be imploring words over and over.

I know it's not the happy ending because it's not ending. The sky changes. The music changes and is not ending. It is not unfinished. It is unending.

About the Author

John Taggart was born in Perry, Iowa, on October 5, 1942. He studied at Earlham College, the University of Chicago, and Syracuse University. While an undergraduate he began editing the poetry magazine *Maps*, continuing until the mid-1970s. From 1969 to 2001 he taught in the English Department and directed the Interdisciplinary Arts Program at Shippensburg University (Pennsylvania). He has received a number of awards for his teaching and writing, among others the Commonwealth Award for Academic Service, the *Chicago Review* poetry prize, and National Endowment for the Arts fellowships. He lives in the Cumberland Valley of south-central Pennsylvania.

Lannan Literary Selections

For two decades Lannan Foundation has supported the
publication and distribution of exceptional literary works.
Copper Canyon Press gratefully acknowledges their support.

LANNAN LITERARY SELECTIONS 2010

Stephen Dobyns, *Winter's Journey*

Travis Nichols, *See Me Improving*

James Richardson, *By the Numbers*

John Taggart, *Is Music: Selected Poems*

Jean Valentine, *Break the Glass*

RECENT LANNAN LITERARY SELECTIONS
FROM COPPER CANYON PRESS

Michael Dickman, *The End of the West*

James Galvin, *As Is*

David Huerta, *Before Saying Any of the Great Words: Selected Poems,*
translated by Mark Schafer

Sarah Lindsay, *Twigs and Knucklebones*

Heather McHugh, *Upgraded to Serious*

W.S. Merwin, *Migration: New & Selected Poems*

Valzhyna Mort, *Factory of Tears,* translated by Franz Wright
and Elizabeth Oehlkers Wright

Taha Muhammad Ali, *So What: New & Selected Poems, 1971–2005,*
translated by Peter Cole, Yahya Hijazi, and Gabriel Levin

Lucia Perillo, *Inseminating the Elephant*

Ruth Stone, *In the Next Galaxy*

Connie Wanek, *On Speaking Terms*

C.D. Wright, *One Big Self: An Investigation*

For a complete list of Lannan Literary Selections from
Copper Canyon Press, please visit Partners on our Web site:

www.coppercanyonpress.org

The Chinese character for poetry is made up of two parts: "word" and "temple." It also serves as pressmark for Copper Canyon Press.

Since 1972, Copper Canyon Press has fostered the work of emerging, established, and world-renowned poets for an expanding audience. The Press thrives with the generous patronage of readers, writers, booksellers, librarians, teachers, students, and funders—everyone who shares the belief that poetry is vital to language and living.

Major funding has been provided by:

Amazon.com

Anonymous

Beroz Ferrell & The Point, LLC

Golden Lasso, LLC

Lannan Foundation

National Endowment for the Arts

Cynthia Lovelace Sears and Frank Buxton

William and Ruth True

Washington State Arts Commission

Charles and Barbara Wright

For information and catalogs:

COPPER CANYON PRESS
Post Office Box 271
Port Townsend, Washington 98368
360-385-4925
www.coppercanyonpress.org

Copper Canyon Press gratefully acknowledges board member Jim Wickwire in honor of his many years of service to poetry and independent publishing.

This book is set in Whitman, developed from Kent Lew's studies of W.A. Dwiggins's Caledonia. The heads are set in Legato, designed by Evert Bloemsma. Book design and composition by Valerie Brewster, Scribe Typography. Printed on archival-quality paper at McNaughton & Gunn, Inc.